Free Trade Reimagined

● ○ ●

ROBERTO MANGABEIRA UNGER

Free Trade Reimagined

● ○ ●

*The World Division of Labor
and the Method of Economics*

PRINCETON UNIVERSITY PRESS
PRINCETON AND OXFORD

Copyright © 2007 by Princeton University Press

Published by Princeton University Press, 41 William Street, Princeton,

New Jersey 08540

In the United Kingdom: Princeton University Press, 3 Market Place,

Woodstock, Oxfordshire OX20 1SY

All Rights Reserved

Library of Congress Cataloging-in-Publication Data

Unger, Roberto Mangabeira.

Free trade reimagined : the world division of labor and the method of

economics / Roberto Mangabeira Unger.

p. cm.

Includes index.

ISBN 978-0-691-13429-1 (hardcover : alk. paper)   1. Economics.   2. Free trade.

3. Free enterprise.   4. Globalization—Economic aspects.   I. Title.

HF1713.U42 2007

382'.71–dc22   2007017229

British Library Cataloging-in-Publication Data is available

This book has been composed in Minion

Printed on acid-free paper. ∞

press.princeton.edu

Printed in the United States of America

1 3 5 7 9 10 8 6 4 2

Contents

● ○ ●

This book stands on its own as an argument about the international division of labor and the method of economics. The reader should nevertheless know that the argument forms part of a larger intellectual program. The program rebels against the tendencies now prevailing in the social sciences and humanities. It seeks alternatives to the arrangements and the assumptions of contemporary societies. It tries to give new meaning to the revolutionary ideas of human liberation and empowerment that, for the last few centuries, have aroused the whole world. It turns thought against fate.

False Necessity (Verso, 2001), *Social Theory: Its Situation and Its Task* (Verso, 2004), and *Plasticity into Power* (Verso, 2004) carry this program forward as a social theory. *What Should Legal Analysis Become?* (Verso, 1996) advances it in the discipline that, together with political economy, provides the most promising tools with which to reimagine the organization of social life. *Democracy Realized: The Progressive Alternative* (Verso, 1998) and *What Should the Left Propose?* (Verso, 2005) develop it as an institutional proposal. *Passion* (Free Press, 1984) and *The Self Awakened: Pragmatism Unbound* (Harvard University Press, 2007) deepen and generalize it as a philosophical conception.*

*For further texts from this intellectual program, see www .robertounger.net.

Free Trade Reimagined

● ○ ●

Themes and Scope of this Book

● ○ ●

The idea of free trade combines theoretical interest with practical significance. It takes us into the heart of economic theory and into the midst of contemporary debates about the world economy. It has become much more than a slogan to conjure with; it has turned into a promise or a menace, a nearly self-evident truth or a source of bafflement, the pride of the hardest of the hard social sciences and the bugbear of those who resist its conclusions.

If countries specialize in what they produce, the whole world can reap the benefits. It is a simple message of enormous power, promising both greater riches and more freedom.

As a subject of theoretical concern, free trade leads into the inner sanctum of economic theorizing. Belief in the gains to be secured through free trade, on the basis of established or constructed comparative advantage, has long been recognized as one of the most counterintuitive and characteristic of the notions of economics. It is a conception embodying the most pervasive theme in economic analysis: the idea of exchange, for reciprocal benefit, among specialized producers in a division of labor and of the market as a form of cooperation among strangers who are neither friends nor enemies and who need only the cold calculus of interest to establish a common practical bond. The deepest source of the appeal of free trade arises from the conviction that it is not a device but rather, as Alfred Marshall claimed, "the absence of any device."

As an issue of practical significance, free trade stands in the middle of contemporary debates about globalization: the emergent world trading system is as much the centerpiece of the present regime of globalization as the doctrine of free trade is the simplest and sharpest expression of economic analysis put to practical use. If we can change what free trade means and how it is organized, we can do the same, more generally, to globalization. And if we can have globalization on our terms, rather than on those of the supposedly irresistible forces that its contemporary form is claimed to represent, all bets are off: we are freer than we suppose to rethink and to reconstruct.

The doctrine of free trade, as it has been understood, is fundamentally defective. Its flaws cannot be remedied by a series of localized qualifications of analysis and policy. The alternative is not to embrace a theory justifying protectionism but rather to reject and to revise the terms on which the debate between free trade and protectionism has long taken place. Such a revision has implications for the method of economics.

The point of largest theoretical significance to emerge from my argument is that a system of free trade will be the more advantageous to those who engage in it (whether or not they are sovereign countries) if it allows them the greatest possible experimental freedom to change their practices and institutions of production. This freedom of revision, however, may conflict with what free trade has traditionally been understood to be and to require.

The point of greatest practical relevance, intimately related to that theoretical conception, is that it makes no sense to organize the world trading system around the goal of maximizing free trade, in the sense in which we are used to defining free trade. A single-minded insistence on the maximization of free trade gives too little weight to an imperative that turns out to be of vital, indeed of increasing significance: the need of every country, richer or poorer, to avoid lasting confinement to a particular place in the international division of labor and to the styles of production, the strategies of development, and the sets of institutions that may exert this confining influence.

If the immediate topic of this book is the contest over free trade and over the form of an open international economy, its ultimate subjects are the world division of labor and the method of economics. We cannot escape the confines of the traditional debate about free trade and protection and do justice to the possibilities of globalization without changing some of our most fundamental assumptions about market economies and the division of labor. That the future of economic growth lies with permanent innovation rather than with the coercive extraction of a social surplus, that freedom experimentally to combine people, ideas, and things must therefore be liberated from all unnecessary institutional restraints and dogmas, that the best market economy is the one that gives the greatest opportunity to the most people in the most ways, that a free economic system must be based on free labor, and that the capacity to use governmental power for the purpose of broadening opportunity can be exercised to advantage only insofar as the state ceases to be in the pocket of privileged and moneyed interests—all these are platitudes of contemporary discourse, embraced with the greatest enthusiasm by those who collaborate with the dictatorship of no alternatives under which the world is now bent.

The words of this litany, however, belong in the mouths of revolutionaries. To think these words through is to revise our ideas concerning what is most important about market economies and the division of labor in the workplace, the national economy, or the whole world. To make these words real is to rebel against the institutions in which market economies and the division of labor remain embodied.

It is an intellectual task for which the present methods of economics are inadequate. It would be tempting to adopt a strategy of caution, insisting that economics, purged of abusive applications and restored to analytic purity, provides help, and imposes no obstacles, to such a campaign. In this book I reject that claim: its modesty does not make up for its falsehood. The practice of economic analysis inaugurated in the late nineteenth century by Walras, Jevons, and Menger, which came to be labeled "marginalism" and which guided the mainstream of subsequent economic theory and culminated in the theory of general equilibrium, is not only insufficient to the execution of the task. It is also, in certain decisive respects, incompatible with it.

If economics continues to swing between purity of analysis, retreating from all controversial explanatory and prescriptive ideas, and abuse of application, unjustifiably equating abstract conceptions like the idea of a market economy with particular contingent sets of economic arrangements, it will not open the way. It will stand in the way. There are many past and present varieties of economic analysis, from the old institutional economics to the new behavioral economics, that suggest different methods and directions. However, they have not developed—and maybe they cannot develop—into ways of dealing with the problems that are central to the argument of this book. Their characteristic inability to imagine the possible forms of economic life cramps their insight into its actual forms.* For these reasons, the attempt here to revise the terms of the traditional controversy about free trade and protection and to reconsider the nature and prospects of the world division of labor leads as well into an argument about the method of economics.

Chapter One explains why there is intellectual as well as practical trouble with the doctrine of free trade. It begins by enumerating a series of puzzles about the nature and benefits of free trade that the development of economic ideas has deepened rather than solved. It goes on to discuss the failure of history to confirm doctrine: never has a practical program enjoyed so much prestige with so little justification in historical experience. It ends by discussing

---

*The "new institutional economics" of the late twentieth century, unlike the German institutional economics or the American institutional economics of the late nineteenth and early twentieth centuries, is not an example of such an arrested departure from the mainstream of thinking. Wedded to ideas of institutional convergence and functionalist determinism, it explains the institutional framework of economic activity, including the institutions of the existing market economies, in a way that makes these arrangements seem the natural or necessary setting of the advanced economies. As a result, it squanders the intellectual opportunity presented by the study of institutions and comes to represent an anti-institutional economics. There are few more striking instances of the right-wing Hegelianism—the real is rational—that pervades the social sciences today.

why a doctrine with feet of clay has been able to cut so imposing a figure in the debates of the modern world.

Chapter Two addresses the intellectual core of the argument for trade: the doctrine of comparative advantage. This doctrine turns out to be incomplete in a series of connected ways. To interpret correctly what it says, we have to combine it with much that it fails to say. The meaning of the part that we have, however, depends on the missing part. Criticism of the theory of comparative advantage leads directly into criticism of the dominant style of economic analysis; latter-day statements of that theory are among the most characteristic expressions of this style.

Chapter Three responds to the incompleteness of the doctrine of comparative advantage. It does so by presenting ideas—about international trade and, more generally, about the market economy and the division of labor—that can do justice to the puzzles and the facts explored in the first two chapters. In particular, these ideas provide building blocks for an approach to free trade. We cannot develop a better approach to free trade—one capable of transcending the conventional terms of the debate between free traders and protectionists—without questioning and revising the premises on which the traditional doctrine relied.

Such assumptions concern some of the most fundamental ideas in economics: the nature of a market economy and of the alternative institutional forms it can take; the reasons why some of the central problems of an economy must be solved outside the economy, in politics, and why the organization of politics is therefore decisive for the character of economic life; the features of a division of labor—in the workplace, in a country, or in the whole world—that are most important to innovation and growth; and the way we should think about the division of labor once we rid ourselves of the tyranny of the ideas for which Adam Smith's pin factory and Henry Ford's assembly line have been made to stand. Rethinking free trade turns out to depend on much more than ideas about commerce.

These views form the backdrop to the development and defense of three theses about free trade advanced in Chapter Four: first, about the economic circumstances in which free trade is likely to be most beneficial or most dangerous; second, about the political circumstances in which restraints on trade are likely to serve broader or narrower interests; and third, about the paradoxical and misunderstood relation among the different ways in which free trade—or, more generally, a free economy—can be free. Taken together, these theses form the elements of a way of thinking about free trade. They also provide the rudiments of an approach to the building of an open world economy. It is a way of thinking that neither reaffirms nor repudiates the traditional commitment to free trade as an indispensable part of the road to global progress. What it has to say cannot be adequately captured within the terms of the familiar disputes between free traders and protectionists.

Chapter Five explores the programmatic implications of the analysis, its consequences for the reformation of the world trading system as well as for the redirection of national development strategies. Free trade forms the kernel of the theory and practice of globalization. We have become accustomed to the idea that all we can do with globalization is to have either more or less of it, or to have it either more slowly or more quickly. The argument of this book leads to the conclusion that we can and should have free trade and globalization on terms different from those in which we now encounter them. We need not merely dose them or pace them; we can rethink and remake them. Ideas alone are powerless to produce such a reorientation. However, we cannot bring it about without ideas.

CHAPTER 1

Troubles: The Enigmas of Free Trade

● ○ ●

Familiar Problems, Disturbing Solutions

I begin by enumerating some familiar problems in the doctrine of free trade conducted on the basis of specialized lines of production within an international division of labor, particularly when such national specializations are motivated by comparative advantage.* These problems—and the solutions that have been proposed for

---

*A country is said to enjoy an absolute advantage over another country in the production of a good if it can produce the good more efficiently, that is, at lower cost, than the other country. It is said to enjoy a comparative advantage over another country in the production of a good if it can produce that good at lower opportunity cost than the other country, that is, with relatively less opportunity to commit the resources it devotes to the production of that good to a more efficient use. A country that fails to have an absolute advantage in the production of a good may nevertheless possess a comparative advantage in it. Comparative advantage vastly expands the basis for international specialization of production. For this reason, and because it is both counterintuitive in its claims and far-reaching in its implications, it has been, ever since its formulation by David Ricardo almost two hundred years ago, the cornerstone of thinking about international trade. The next chapter deals at length with the doctrine of comparative advantage. The distinction between absolute and comparative advantage is largely irrelevant to the puzzles listed immediately below, although comparative rather than absolute advantage would ordinarily be regarded as the main field for their application. Thus, I use in the following list the simple term "advantage."

them—have not been thought to discredit either the central insight of the doctrine or its programmatic consequence, the beneficence of free trade. Indeed, they do not. They nevertheless pose a challenge that contemporary thinking about trade and free trade has yet adequately to meet. How, why, and with what result the force of this challenge has continued to be evaded is a matter requiring further reflection. Consider a brief, nonexhaustive list of these long-recognized objections and complications.

1. The assumption of a uniquely efficient assignment of productive specializations among countries in an international division of labor: who is to produce what. Even if we assume that comparative advantage is a given rather than a construction (see the next proposition on this list), it is more realistic to suppose that there are alternative sets of efficient assignments of advantage among economies, just as there are multiple ways any economy can be in equilibrium, each with different consequences for national welfare and growth. The less that advantage is determined by nature, the greater is likely to be the significance of the problem of multiple efficient solutions to the allocation of specialized national roles in world trade. Each such allocation will have distinct results for both welfare and growth.

2. The assumption that advantage is given rather than made. This assumption becomes less tenable as we move away from natural advantage. The most tangible example of made advantage is the development of economies of scale and scope, as well as of concentrations of skill, in a line of business in which a country may have had no natural advantage. However, once the principle is admitted that advantage can be deliberately created by governmental initiative and collective action, it applies to every reason for a country's practical success or failure, including its institutions and practices, social and political as well as economic. Trade theory has had difficulty coming to terms with how the construction of advantage occurs, for the same reason that economics in general has had trouble dealing with how the institutional and psychological assumptions of maximizing behavior in a market economy are established and modified.

3. The assumption that it is tenable to foreclose the two previous sets of concerns by saying that either advantage, when not given by nature, will be generated by market activity itself or that it will be produced by governmental intervention, with all its attendant risks (playing favorites, riding hobbyhorses). In fact, advantage has always been shaped by a combination of private enterprise and public action. As soon as we acknowledge this fact, however, we realize that there is no closed set of possible institutional forms of such a combination. Indeed, there is no single and uncontroversial institutional achievement of worldwide free trade.

The concept of a market economy is institutionally indeterminate. That is to say, it is capable of being realized in different legal and institutional directions, each with dramatic consequences for every aspect of social life, including the class structure of society and the distribution of wealth and power. The idea of a universal regime of free trade is institutionally indeterminate in the same sense and for the same reasons. Which of its institutional realizations prevails has immense importance for the future of humanity. These debates cannot be captured within the categories of long-standing controversies about free trade and protection.

4. The assumption that so long as we correct market imperfections (according to the formula of first, fix them; if not, compensate for them by a domestic initiative; only as a final resort, impose a restraint on trade), we can move from the static efficiency of free trade to its intertemporal efficiency and from its intertemporal efficiency to its beneficial effect on economic growth. In fact, the first link holds only if intertemporal efficiency is defined so narrowly as to deprive it of theoretical or practical interest, and the second link (as the later observations about historical experience confirm) is nonexistent.

Moreover, the language of market imperfections, as applied to the "infant industry" and "monopoly power in trade" arguments for protection, trivializes the central point: not how to reestablish the market or what to do when the market fails, but what kind of market—on the basis of what institutions and practices—to establish in the first place. We cannot reach this point by focusing solely on advantage, whether given or made; on the contrary, the analysis of advantage presupposes that we have already disposed of this issue to our satisfaction. We have not.

5. The assumption that a country's trade policy should not be influenced by the willingness of its trading partners to abolish or to diminish restraints on trade. The traditional view (against which strategic trade theory staged a limited revolt) has been that although real-world departures from this assumption may justify circumstantial resort to reciprocity and retaliation, they do not compromise the case for a trade regime that is as universal and as free as possible.

6. If, however, the whole system of world trade and all the institutions and practices by which it is realized in any given historical circumstance are both particular and contingent, if they are incapable of being inferred by pure analysis from the idea of free trade, if they are the products of shifting conflicts of interest and vision on the world stage, if they therefore deeply bear the imprint of everyone's strategies, and if the strategies of a few preponderant economic powers are likely to be decisive in determining their content, then the assumption that a country's trade policy should be independent of the trade concessions it wins from the countries with which it trades makes little sense. Strategic trade theory failed to go far enough in resisting it.

A puzzle will occur to any reader of this book who has studied the history of debates about free trade and protection. Everything in this short list of ambiguities and flaws in the traditional doctrine of free trade based on comparative or absolute advantage is well known. The interest of the list lies in combining the ideas that constitute the list, in deepening and generalizing them, and in grasping their unrecognized implications. The student of the controversy about free trade, however, will object that the history of this debate has been largely preoccupied with beliefs of an entirely different order. To these beliefs the propositions in the short list bear no self-evident relation.

Traditional objections to free trade can be broadly placed into two categories. In one category are the arguments concerning the special instances in which restraints on trade may be justified because of the failure to solve what today we would describe as a collective-action problem in the development of a regime of universal free trade. If markets are not universally open, it may not, under certain conditions, be in the interest of every trading party to act as if they were; that is, it may not be in its interest to offer its trading partners a unilateral and unreciprocated abolition of restraints on trade. This claim was the nub of Robert Torrens's "terms of trade" argument.

It is an argument that has always invited a twofold response from the defenders of free trade as it is conventionally understood. One response emphasizes how special are the conditions under which restraint may be more advantageous than unreciprocated protection. The other response insists that the actual practice of protection is likely to squander its theoretical benefits by lending itself to the service of powerful interests and fashionable dogmas.

In a second category are the arguments dealing with the perverse distributive effects of free trade in a particular situation, including both distribution among sectors of the economy and distribution among classes of society. In this second category fall Frank Graham's "increasing returns argument" (according to which if manufacturing is subject to increasing returns to scale and agriculture to decreasing returns to scale, a country importing manufactured goods and specializing in agriculture may have reason to impose a tariff on manufactures in order to encourage a shift to the higher-productivity sector, with its increasing returns to scale), Mihail Manoïlescu's related "wage differential argument" (according to which developing countries might be justified in imposing restraints on trade to encourage the movement of labor from low-wage, low-productivity agriculture to high-wage, high-productivity industry), James Bristock Bridgen's so-called Australian argument (according to which restraints on trade might be justified for countries whose factor endowments were such that, although facing diminishing returns in agriculture, they continued to specialize in the world economy as agricultural exporters), and the Stolper-Samuelson theorem (according to which an import tariff may raise the real income of labor and reduce the real income of capital when the import-substituting sector produces a labor-intensive good).

The common element in these arguments of the second category is the claim that, under the special conditions each of them stipulates, free trade may produce a redistribution of gains among sectors of production or among classes of society that is economically inconvenient as well as socially undesirable because it inhibits a national economy from climbing the ladder of productivity more quickly.

Both sets of arguments address circumstances in which, for particular reasons, the case for free trade may fail to persuade. They provide no basis for resisting trade beyond those circumstances or for revising our view of its benefits. They thus reinforce John Stuart Mill's contention that "the protectionist doctrine finds support in some particular cases"—and only in such cases.

The result is to provoke from the defenders of the doctrine of free trade a response that has succeeded in robbing these objections from the competitive assumptions or the distributive effects of freer trade of much of their theoretical and practical force. The response comes in two parts. The first part is to interpret each of the arguments as the description of a low-productivity trap. The way out of the trap, the votaries of free trade say, is not to restrict openness in the global market; it is to radicalize openness—competition, flexibility, and capability through education, training, and benchmarking—in the domestic market. The second part is to suggest that so long as market failure persists, the short-term antidote to its perverse distributive consequences should be a corrective or compensatory transfer of resources. Restraint on trade should be a last resort; it is likely to be the most costly solution, and its costs are likely to be magnified by the foothold it provides for the ravages of favoritism and dogmatism.

So it is that the two familiar sets of objections to the doctrine of free trade conducted on the basis of comparative advantage can be quickly and effectively circumscribed. The doctrine is general; the objections are particular. Because they are particular, they invite particular responses that leave the essentials of the doctrine untouched.

Now return to the earlier summary list of analytical conundrums. They are not particular; they are general. They reveal difficulties or ambiguities in the conception itself, not just in its application to specific circumstances. They suggest that free trade—the international division of labor, the global trading regime—might have different meanings and be organized in different ways, with different consequences. They imply that instead of choosing more or less free trade, we might think of free trade in a different manner and organize it accordingly.

The problems on the short list therefore enjoy a conceptual priority to the two families of practical arguments—about collective action and about distribution—that have occupied so much of the historical controversy about free trade and protection. Until we have solved these problems, we cannot know with assurance what to make of those well-known arguments. Is there a way of conceiving, developing, and organizing an open world economy that prevents countries from falling into low-productivity traps like those described by Graham, Manoïlescu, and Bridgen? Can the problem of collective action in the construction of such an open world economy be solved in a way that enables countries to diverge, even increasingly, in their forms of economic organization as well as in their lines of business?

A central theme runs through the preceding discussion of the conundrums latent in the conception of free trade and of the matters left unresolved by the historical debates about protectionism. The theme is the need for a contest among ways of imagining and of organizing worldwide free trade. The significance of the conundrums is to suggest that there is room to rethink international free trade and therefore also room to reorganize it. The meaning of the history of the debates is that until we determine what our intellectual and practical alternatives are in that larger struggle, we cannot bring those debates to a close, or even assign them a definitive meaning.

There is no single uncontroversial realization of the idea of a universal regime of free trade. To take a simple example, will it be free trade of goods with mobility of labor or free trade of goods without mobility of labor? So long as there are different possible futures, including different possible futures of free trade itself, there will be different strategies among its participants, committed by reason of interest and vision to one such future against others. Strategizing is not what takes place when free trade ends. A regime of free trade is not a perpetual-motion machine that, once established, absolves us of further institutional choices and strategic conflicts.

The common and combined effect of these problems is to require the qualification and the expansion of traditional free trade doctrine. The movement to save the doctrine from the objections will not be persuasive and successful unless it goes in a particular direction. This direction emphasizes the multiplicity of possible successful assignments of productive specializations among countries. It also underlines the role of governments and firms in making new comparative advantage. Multiplicity rather than singularity of opportunity and response; advantage and capability as achieved rather than as given, as goals rather than as guides—these are the characteristic themes of plausible answers to those objections.

What emerges from such answers is a way of responding to the five problems I have just enumerated that disposes of them by doing just the opposite of what has been the main tendency of economic theorizing for the last hundred and twenty years. The response disposes of these problems only by undermining the idea of the market (in this case the world market realized through universal trade) as a perpetual-motion machine that can define its own presuppositions and pick out uniquely efficient solutions to the problems of resource allocation. It disposes of them only by weakening the contrast between the effort to find the most efficient (or even Pareto-improving, that is to say better for everyone) solution within the given framework and then by reinventing the framework. And it therefore disposes of them only by connecting economics and politics rather than by keeping them carefully and anxiously apart.

Consider, for example, the substitution of the idea of constructed comparative advantage for the idea of established comparative advantage. Once we acknowledge that comparative advantage can be, and always has been, shaped by governmental initiative and collective action as well as by private enterprise, we have to ask which features of a trading system may either encourage or inhibit such restless tilting of the scales. Once we combine the idea of constructed comparative advantage with the idea of multiple answers to the question of who may be the most efficient producer of what in the world economy, we begin to tear down the wall between the debate about how to understand and how to organize universal free trade and the struggle over the content of the development strategies different countries should embrace. And once we admit that the institutional indeterminacy of the market concept—our inability to infer a particular legal and institutional organization of the market from the abstract idea of a market—is aggravated by the institutional indeterminacy of the idea of global free trade—the possibility of interpreting the legal and institutional implications of this idea in sharply divergent ways—we begin to wonder what it is that we embrace when we commit to free trade.

So each of the well-known objections I have listed yields to answers that are almost as familiar. However, the cumulative effect of these answers is to make the theoretical meaning and the practical significance of the doctrine of free trade depend on ideas about much more. My argument expands into empirical and normative controversy rather than retreating from it. In this sense, it devalues the autonomy of economic analysis rather than enhance it. It goes in a direction opposite to the direction that economic theory has on the whole taken. It uses trouble to create, through more trouble, insight.

The History of Free Trade and Protection: Subversive Lessons

There has never been a more astonishing contrast between the intellectual prestige of a social or economic doctrine and the weakness of its vindication by historical experience than the influence enjoyed by the idea of the advantages of universal free trade, in the face of facts that seem to contradict this idea.

Any fair-minded reading of the historical record shows that there is no evidence for a consistent or general positive relation between free trade and economic growth. There is more than a little evidence for the supposition that they have often been negatively related. I do not take this evidence to justify a systematic bias toward trade protection; indeed, it is a central tenet of the argument of this essay that the terms of the traditional debate about free trade and protection are and continue to be ill-conceived. It is impossible to achieve intellectual clarity so long as we stubbornly rely on misreadings of the historical record. The facts at issue are not obscure; they do not depend on research into as yet unvisited archives or on convoluted interpretations of hermetic texts. They are as simple and straightforward as we can ever expect a set of complex historical events, over extended time, to be.

For much of the nineteenth and twentieth centuries—until the present episode of globalization began in earnest in the closing decades of the last century—the rich countries of the North Atlantic world were a stronghold of protectionism. The most notable exception was the pioneering industrial power, Great Britain. By contrast, free trade, based on established comparative advantage, prevailed, by a combination of political imposition and ideological submission, in much of the poorer rest of the world.

In continental Europe, a protectionist bias prevailed for most of the nineteenth century. It became strongest in the period from 1892 to 1914. This was the heyday of the previous episode of globalization—the one that came before the globalizing impulse of the late twentieth and the early twenty-first centuries. The most notable movement toward free trade took place in the years following the Anglo-French trade treaty of 1861. It is striking that this turn to free trade persisted during the period of the great European depression of the 1870s, an economic downturn in some respects more severe than the depression of the 1930s.

No Western country professed a more long-standing and radical devotion to protectionism than the one that was destined to become the leading economic power in the world, the United

States. The sole consistent opposition to this bias came from the slaveholding South. The doctrinal formulation of the protectionist bias in Henry Carey's "American System" predated the formulation of the ideas of Friedrich List.

The periods of moderation of protectionism—the years after the Democrat Party came to power in 1844 and after the Underwood Tariff of 1913—were brief in duration and limited in reach. It is especially interesting that the protectionist impulse strengthened rather than waned after the United States had already achieved its status as a leading industrial economy in the late nineteenth century. The emphasis of argument shifted from infant industries to wage protection and aggressive national strategy.

Some may conjecture that the United States and continental Europe would have done even better had they taken the path urged on them by the English proponents of free trade and comparative advantage and by their liberal disciples abroad. Such a counterfactual conjecture, however, would amount to sheer dogmatic fantasy; it lies beyond the reach of proof or falsification.

In most of what was later to be described as the third world, especially the countries under the outright control or the economic and political influence of the North Atlantic powers, free trade, justified by a simplified liberal and Ricardian discourse, reigned supreme. Two very clear examples of its application were to be found in some of the major countries of Latin America (especially Brazil) and the Ottoman Empire. On the whole and for most of time, these same regions of the world grew very slowly under the long dominion of the free-trading doctrine.

There is no basis to infer from these facts, in which so many other circumstances intervened, a simple inverse relation between free trade and economic growth. They nevertheless cast doubt on the thesis of a positive relation of economic growth to free trade. Not only can no negative relation between economic growth and restraints on trade be established, for much of modern history it is hard even to demonstrate a negative relation between protection and an increase in trade flows. Many countries expanded their share of world trade, and the importance of their own trade flows relative to their own GDP, during those times when they increased trade protection.

Let us stand back for a moment from the narrower controversy about free trade and protection and consider the lessons of the equivocal historical experience. These lessons will help inform a view outreaching the terms of that debate.

A first lesson is that the lowering of trade barriers has ordinarily followed rather than preceded the achievement of high and sustained growth. Ascendant countries have characteristically joined the trading system and then lowered their defenses, in stepwise fashion and on terms compatible with a particular strategy and vision. They have practiced, *avant la lettre*, active rather than passive engagement with the world economy.

A second lesson is that even before they achieved high and sustained growth the countries most resolute and successful in practicing relatively unrestricted free trade have often been small commercial entrepots. They have drawn their economic lifeblood from privileged relations to a much larger—and much more trade-protected—economy. A contemporary example is Hong Kong. A historical instance is provided by the Hanseatic free cities. Their established comparative advantage was geography, combined with created institutional arrangements and cultural predispositions that helped them make best use of their geographic setting.

A third lesson is that many countries successful in a niche—a line of specialized production within the world economy—have then failed to reinvent themselves when circumstances required them to do so. The institutions, practices, and beliefs fostering this capacity for continued reinvention turn out to be more important than any particular success or niche. A particular and elusive dialectic between protection and free trade has played an important role in sustaining these conditions of the collective capacity for self-reinvention.

A fourth lesson is that the most successful countries, regions, and networks of firms have ordinarily been those that are able to pillage the world for resources, technologies, and ideas while maintaining independent centers of decision. Such economies have managed to enhance and safeguard the ability to do things their way. The particular level of free trade and protection they practiced may often have been much less important than the way in which each of them understood and implemented free trade and protection, such as by providing for protection but with massive use of foreign capital to develop the national infrastructure (as in mid-nineteenth-century United States) or by increasing free trade but with avoidance of foreign control of major enterprises (as in mid-twentieth-century Japan, Korea, and Taiwan).

The division of the world into sovereign nation-states has proved to be one way of creating a basis for such fertile divergence. If there were a truly global economy, with borderless trade, we would have reason to find a functional substitute for what sovereign states, deploying selective free trade and selective protection, have achieved.

Contemporary experience suggests one major addition to these historical inferences. If there is a lesson to be drawn from the record of success and failure in national development in the twentieth century, it is a conclusion that may at first appear to be paradoxical. The apparent paradox comes in two parts.

The turn to the market—to a national market economy and to the world market—has indeed worked. However, it has worked best when countries and their governments and thinkers have been bold in organizing a market economy and in providing for national engagement in the world economy on their own terms, often through unfamiliar institutions or unfamiliar combinations of familiar arrangements.

What has counted in the turn to the national and world market has never been acquiescence in a dogmatic institutional formula about the proper form of a market economy. It has never been acceptance of the simple-minded promises made by the doctrine of free trade on the basis of given comparative advantage. It has been some measure of success in an effort to reconcile two commitments. One commitment has been to decentralize economic power and opportunity and to expand the scale and scope of markets. The other commitment has been actively to reshape established comparative advantage through governmental initiative and collective action as well as through private enterprise, thus preserving the vital capacity for national defiance and divergence. So it is, for example, that China has advanced, even in the midst of unbroken despotism and mounting inequality, while Latin America, the most obedient of all contemporary regions of the world to the pseudo-orthodoxy of the market turn, has suffered a catastrophic decline in its relative position in the global economy.

The Authority of Free Trade Doctrine: Reasons Amounting to Objections

How could a conception such as the traditional teaching of free trade, compromised by such serious and numerous fallacies and contradicted by so much historical experience, enjoy such daunting intellectual authority? The answers to this question are of more than intellectual-historical interest. They allow us to understand what is at stake in the debate about free trade and comparative advantage and to escape the confines of the traditional discussion. Here are four reasons why that doctrine has commanded so much authority on so little basis.

A first source of the appeal of the doctrine is its intimate but equivocal relation to the idea of efficient resource allocation within a market. The notion of the Pareto-improving character of an international division of labor (that is, a division of labor creating more gains for all trading partners than would some preexisting assignment of productive specializations among countries), organized according to given comparative advantage and realized through free trade, may seem at first uncontroversial. It appears simply to work out, in international trade, the general idea of market-oriented exchange. Yet, from such a seemingly uncontroversial starting point, it generates results that have been described as among the most unexpected in social science. It combines a commitment to a widely accepted, even venerable postulate and a power to upset prejudice and to cause surprise. This combination lends to free trade doctrine a seductive aura reminiscent of the charms of mathematical discovery.

The translation of the general idea of market-based allocation into the doctrine of free trade on the basis of established or constructed comparative advantage reveals a general feature of the style of economic theorizing that has come to prevail since the rise of marginalism. The idea of the market as a perpetual-motion machine, able to allocate resources to their most efficient uses, remains immune to empirical or normative attack only so long as it also remains empty of explanatory or prescriptive consequence. The greater its analytic purity, the weaker is its power to explain or to guide. It achieves its power by its admixture with causal ideas and normative assumptions that it must borrow from other bodies of thought.

The workings of free trade doctrine illustrate this dilemma of purity and sterility. The idea of market allocation through an international division of labor acquires definite meaning and force only by relying on controversial assumptions that are crucially incomplete. The more we come to see comparative advantage as made rather than given—made by political initiative and collective action outside the market, as well as by the standard forms of market behavior—the less the doctrine, in its narrow and conventional form, makes sense. If comparative advantage becomes the standard by which to assess the merits of any given assignment of productive specializations among countries, we cannot know for sure to what alternative assignments we should compare the existing assignment.

Another example is the view of the alternative institutional forms that a market economy may take. The assumptions about property and contract, or about the relative cross-border mobility of different factors of production, or about the ways in which governmental initiative and private enterprise may interact are not minor details; they go to the heart of the free trade program. We cannot infer answers to the questions they pose from the abstract concepts of the market or of free trade. We must ground those answers in contentious causal or normative views.

A second source of the prestige of the free trade teaching has to do with the relation among intellectual life, power politics, and historical experience. The periods in which free trade theory has enjoyed its greatest influence have been those in which intellectuals in the leading powers of the day have felt greatest confidence in the world order those powers sponsored. Free trade has been merely an aspect, if an important one, of those cosmopolitan projects. It has promised to give the cosmopolitanism of the moment support and consequence in the hard, tangible realities of commerce.

Conversely, the times in which the hold of free trade doctrine has weakened have been those in which intellectuals in the leading powers have lost confidence in the ability of those powers to shape the world order. It was in such a situation that Keynes in the 1920s underwent his apostasy from the liberal and Ricardian teaching about free trade. In the course of modern history, moments of loss of faith in the power of the hegemons to consummate the marriage of hegemony and cosmopolitanism have been uncommon.

A different and more persistent, but less audible and less prestigious, resistance has emerged from two other quarters. It has come from practical economists and publicists in emerging but still peripheral powers in the imperial order, for example, Henry Carey in mid-nineteenth-century America and Friedrich List in mid-nineteenth-century Germany. It has come as well from the thinkers of backward countries still far removed from the prospect of achieving rich country and world power status, such as the dependency theorists of the 1960s and 1970s in Latin America.

However, these seats of resistance were no match for the teachings of respected intellectual authorities in the imperial centers of the world. The first group of potential resisters were in the process of acquiring a share in the imperial mantle. The second group found themselves relegated for an indefinite time to the outer circles of an intellectual and political purgatory.

A third source of the influence of free trade ideas is the familiar association between selectivity in trade policy, or indeed in any branch of policy, and the capture of governmental power by private interests. We have been repeatedly taught that although governments cannot choose winners, losers can choose governments.

The champions of free trade ideas have been able to claim that rent-seeking behavior feasts on protectionism.

Their claim is not unfounded. Any form of selectivity in the design of law and policy, including trade law and policy, can provide opportunities for the extraction from the state of favors that wound the public interest. In so doing, it may limit economic growth and redistribute to successful rent seekers whatever growth occurs. However, this undisputed fact is not the end of a story; it is only the beginning of a story, as later parts of the argument of this essay seek to establish.

The extent to which governmental power is susceptible to capture by private interests—or to seduction by untested and unfounded dogma—is not a constant, an eternal law of the relations between the government and the economy. It is a variable, shaped by the organization of politics. It is a variable in the same sense that the distortion of markets by asymmetries of power and information is a variable; the former variable is at least as pliant as the latter to conscious institutional design and policy experiment, or simply to the variations of historical experience. If we could have a state less vulnerable to manipulation by powerful special interests and a policymaking practice less inclined to suppress decentralized experiments in the name of imposed schemes, we might have more selectivity in trade policy with less danger. The nature and transformation of politics help determine the limits of the possible in the economy.

A fourth source of the magnetism of free trade doctrine is the power of the political hopes concealed within its prosaic frame. Remember the political emphasis in David Ricardo's canonical statement of the theory of free trade and comparative advantage: "Under a system of perfectly free commerce each country naturally devotes its capital and labor to such employments as are most beneficial to each. By stimulating industry, by rewarding ingenuity, and by using efficaciously the peculiar powers bestowed by nature, it distributes labor most effectively and economically; while, by increasing the general mass of productions, it diffuses benefit, and binds together, by one common interest and intercourse, the universal society of nations throughout the civilized world"

(*On the Principles of Political Economy and Taxation*, Chapter VII, "On Foreign Trade").

The theme of trade as a union of interests capable of smothering or diluting the passions of national glory and power had been a familiar idea for at least several generations before Ricardo wrote. The Ricardian conception of open commerce on the basis of comparative advantage added a vital twist: common sense and material interest, although relatively uncontroversial, would lend support to a project of untrammeled commercial intercourse among nations that was much contested. Once the controversial implications of free trade acquired the authority and the solidity of the much less controversial premises, we would all find a way of buying and selling instead of making war or lighting ideological fires.

Free trade liberalism not only seemed less dangerous than pre-liberal mercantilism, it also held out the prospect of helping to get beyond the savage and inconclusive contest of national rivalries, further aroused and poisoned by wars of religion and of ideology. Commercial interest would do more than foster economic growth, it would serve civilization. It would help establish intercourse and peace on a basis more solid than philosophy, fear, and fellow feeling. Free trade among nations would be a way of agreeing to disagree. It is impossible to contemplate the contemporary rhetorical expressions and political uses of the doctrine I study here without concluding that this view still lives.

The truth, however, is that the organization of an open world economy is not a way of getting beyond the controversies of modern politics. It is just one more theater in which to express and develop them. The attempt to claim for a particular system of free trade a neutrality it does not deserve makes no contribution to world peace and reconciliation. On the contrary, disguising a contentious global project as simple common sense is asking for trouble.

CHAPTER 2

Troubles: The Incompleteness of Comparative Advantage

● ○ ●

The Doctrine of Comparative Advantage

We must go further into the core of the beliefs that have informed and guided the doctrine of free trade if we are to find a point of departure for more reliable insight. This task provides an opportunity to reconsider, through an analysis of this doctrine, both our ideas about the world division of labor and our assumptions about the method of economics. To radicalize the organized anarchy and the restless experimentalism that have played so large a part in the ideal of market economy, rendered worldwide through free trade—at the cost of overturning the institutional and conceptual obstacles that continue to circumscribe them—is the impulse animating my argument.

David Ricardo's idea of comparative advantage—refined, amplified, and qualified by subsequent thinking—stands at the center of those market-respecting beliefs. Reassessing that idea and its theoretical sequels must form part of the effort to lay the groundwork for a different way of thinking. The idea of comparative advantage has been rightly represented as a star example of the achievements of economic analysis; it is an idea that has proved to be at once fertile and counterintuitive.

The reassessment I propose does not deny the power of the concept of comparative advantage and of the tradition of theory that has developed it. It does nevertheless suggest a change of its place in theory and policy. The nub of the problem lies in what the doctrine of comparative advantage leaves unsaid, and more generally in what remains beyond the reach of established economic analysis. The problem lies as well in the surprising results to which we are driven when we try to combine the truth this doctrine reveals with the equally important truths left unexplored. The incompleteness of the doctrine will turn out to be a more formidable obstacle to understanding than is often supposed, and the attempt to redress it will require us to confront and revise much else in our inherited ideas.

"If a foreign country can supply us with a commodity cheaper than we ourselves can make it, better buy it of them with some part of the produce of our own industry, employed in a way in which we have some advantage." So wrote Adam Smith (*The Wealth of Nations,* book IV, section ii, 12), stating the mild and relatively uncontroversial concept of absolute advantage. Ricardo's disturbing innovation was to show that the logic of national specialization of production applied far beyond the terrain of this simple contrast. Comparative advantage, he argued, is enough to justify specialization in production. In our present-day vocabulary we say that a country enjoys comparative advantage in the production of a good if it is able to produce that good at a lower opportunity cost than another country.

Suppose, in Ricardo's canonical example, the presence of only two countries, England and Portugal, and only two goods, wine and cloth, with labor as the sole input in the production of each. Imagine further that Portugal can produce both cloth and wine more efficiently—at lower cost in terms of labor input—than England, but it can produce wine even more efficiently—at lower cost in terms of labor input, relative to England, than it can produce cloth. At first, on principles of absolute advantage, it may seem that Portugal should trade with England in neither wine nor cloth.

Ricardo showed, against the bias of our intuitions, that under the highly restrictive but nevertheless illuminating assumptions of his argument, trade in both wine and cloth, on the basis of specialized production in England and Portugal, would be beneficial to both countries. For each country to receive the greatest possible gain from trade, Portugal should produce only what it is relatively most efficient at producing, wine, and England should produce only what it is relatively least inefficient in producing, cloth. Producing only cloth, England should buy all its wine from Portugal. Both England and Portugal would end up better off than they would otherwise be.

The opportunity cost in Ricardo's example is the amount of wine that must be given up to produce one more unit of cloth. If England must give up less wine to produce another unit of cloth than Portugal must give up cloth to produce another unit of wine, England will enjoy comparative advantage in the production of cloth. Let England produce only cloth, as Portugal produces only wine. By the alchemy of free trade, both will end up with the potential to consume both more cloth and more wine than they would otherwise consume, implementing a "Pareto-optimal improvement," which makes both countries better off than they would otherwise be. Both trading partners stand to improve the situation they would face if either trading partner had rejected or qualified this course of specialization.

Generalized, and enhanced by the refinements and debates of subsequent theorizing, the idea of comparative advantage supplies the kernel of a justification for universal free trade on the basis of productive specialization. Of course, it may be conceded that this justification is incomplete: its force depends, as always in practical economic analysis, on the limiting assumptions on which it relies. It depends as well on the ways in which we choose to compensate, conceptually and practically, for the failure of any or all of these assumptions to hold in fact. However, everything in thought is incomplete; our task, the friends of the doctrine will insist, is to contend with the implications of the incompleteness without betraying the central insight or the path to the enrichment of mankind that this insight opens up. It is a justification that remains plausible until we begin to look further into the consequences of any attempt to combine what the doctrine of comparative advantage says with what it leaves unsaid.

It is true that the theory of comparative advantage and the whole standard form of economic analysis to which it belongs are not, narrowly considered, incompatible with any of the ideas about trade developed in this essay. Nor do they conflict with the broader project of explanation, criticism, and proposal that these ideas exemplify. However, the conclusion that there is no conflict depends on interpreting the doctrine of comparative advantage with sufficient analytic purity and austerity. When the doctrine is interpreted in the larger and looser sense in which it has been generally understood and deployed (and on which its worldly value depends), a conflict emerges. The conflict joined on this wider ground has much to tell us about the character and limitations of postmarginalist economics as a whole, as well as about the insights and illusions of the teaching of free trade in particular. This teaching has often been seen as the crown jewel of economics and as the most persuasive example of its capacity for practical application.

Incompleteness: Indeterminacy Resulting from Failure to Justify Unique Assignments of Comparative Advantage*

The doctrine of comparative advantage is incomplete in three distinct but connected ways. We cannot properly reckon with the intellectual implications of this incompleteness without changing how we think about international trade and ultimately about market-based exchange and the division of labor—primary concerns of economic analysis.

The first species of incompleteness is incompleteness as a result of the failure to arrive at a single, market-clearing solution to the problem of how to organize productive specialization among particular trading partners. Once we go beyond the simple stipulations of Ricardo's famous example, with two commodities and two countries, with homogeneous technology and labor, or beyond the assumptions of the classic form of the more recent

*I thank Sanjay Reddy for criticism and suggestions in the improvement of this section.

Heckscher-Ohlin model, with two commodities, two countries, two inputs to production (such as capital and labor), and knowledge freely shared throughout the world, we shall often find that there are multiple solutions, or infinite solutions, or no solutions at all to the assignment of comparative advantage, that is, the distribution among countries of specializations in production that maximizes each country's gains from trade. (Ricardo's original argument, unlike much subsequent theorizing, depends crucially on differences in the production technologies available to different countries and, as a consequence, on the productivity of their workers.) Moreover, even when there is a unique solution, it often will not be possible to characterize this solution in a straightforward way; it may, for instance, entail that the basket of exports of a country contain a certain average content with respect to the inputs of the production process but tell us little about how that average content is to be achieved.

Whether we fail to reach a unique solution, and in which way, will depend on the manner in which we relax the restrictive assumptions of Ricardo's case in acknowledgment of the complications of reality. The failure of models of international trade always to entail unique, informative market-clearing solutions limits their explanatory power. Further, whether or not a unique market-clearing solution exists, we may be unable to guarantee that the outcomes resulting from international trade belong to a special class of such solutions, those that are described as Pareto-improving because they make all the trading partners they touch better off than the partners would otherwise be. In some instances there may be multiple (or infinite) solutions but the entire "solution set" may consist of possible international production allocations that generate gains of trade for all parties, although varying from solution to solution in the extent and distribution of the gains among the parties. In other instances, most notably when there are increasing returns to scale, some possible production allocations among countries may entail losses from trade, not just for particular firms but also for entire economies.

This problem (of the potential instability of the core results of the theory, in the face of different ways of realizing its assumptions) is no novelty; how to deal with it has been the staple of trade theory, in the tradition of more or less canonical thinking about comparative advantage, for close to a hundred years. Although mainstream theory has been chiefly accustomed to marvel at the supposed robustness of the tenets of one or another model of thinking about comparative advantage under circumstances more complicated than those envisaged by the standard models, the informal objections have origins in the nineteenth century.

The trouble begins immediately with the very first signs of complication. It has long been recognized that as soon as there are more than two countries or two commodities, as, of course, there always will be, there may be multiple solutions (on some further assumptions about the facts), or infinite solutions (on other assumptions), or no solutions (on still other assumptions). When there are multiple or infinite solutions, it will not always be possible to rank them in relation to each other on the basis of criteria supplied to us by the world of ideas within which the doctrine of comparative advantage moves. These criteria are in any event inadequate.

Comparative advantage deals in the coin of static efficiency. It tells us nothing about the adjacent possible in the history of technological and organizational innovation or of economic growth—the next steps we are able to take, in a given time and place, with the materials at hand. What new products and ways of producing them are feasible? Which of the possibilities of specialization suggested by the multiple solutions are more fertile in the opening up of next steps in growth and innovation? Which encourage linkages or analogies to form among whole sets of lines of production or of the technologies and practices they employ? Which, by making demands on the national economy that lie beyond, but not too far beyond, the horizon of present capabilities, destabilize and incite without frustrating? Which most decisively shift the focus of time, energy, and attention away from the productive activities that we already know how to repeat, and therefore also know how to embody in formulas and machines, toward those that we are not yet capable of repeating?

Until we vastly enrich the line of reasoning in which we deploy the idea of comparative advantage, we shall lack any basis on which to choose among the multiple solutions to the problems of productive specialization. We shall find ourselves confronted with the task not simply to know more, but to know something of a different order.

We may well suspect that new information and insight, although acquired for the sake of choosing among the solutions suggested by the unenriched analysis of comparative advantage, might soon lead us to identify available or accessible comparative advantages of which we had been unaware. The distinction between choosing among the identified solutions to the assignment of productive specialization among economies and identifying new solutions to that problem would then begin to collapse.

Also known but less often remarked and yet more disconcerting is the indeterminacy that may result from any shift in the relative costs of the necessary inputs to the production of a good or service that is a candidate to enjoy comparative advantage, or in the relation between the value of the inputs and the value of the output. Labor—the sole factor of production in Ricardo's example—will be combined with other factors of production to make things—call them inputs—that are then used to produce other things—call them outputs. Small shifts in the values of these inputs relative to one another or to the values of the outputs may have radical effects on comparative advantage. Such effects will often seem disproportionate to their causes, like the small flaws of a hero in a Greek tragedy leading relentlessly to catastrophe. They may be difficult to assess and to contain. The consequence may be something between multiplicity and chaos (mathematically speaking) in the analysis of comparative advantage. The multiplication of possible solutions to the problem of identifying comparative advantage will then recur with a vengeance, and the knowledge needed to choose among these solutions will once again be likely to reshape our understanding of what the choices are as well as of their relative merits.

Consider now a series of objections to this complaint of incompleteness of the doctrine of comparative advantage by reason of indeterminacy. Each objection requires a qualification of the doctrine that also deepens it. The outcome is not to withdraw the complaint but to press it yet further.

A preliminary objection is that the statement of the complaint fails properly to distinguish between the external and the internal indeterminacy of thinking about comparative advantage. External indeterminacy is the embarrassing surfeit of different models for the analysis of comparative advantage, each of them making very different and even incompatible assumptions (for example, about the worldwide availability of the same technologies of production) yet all marshaled to the justification of the same practical goal—the advancement of free trade. Internal indeterminacy is the existence, within each of these models, of multiple solutions to the assignment of comparative advantage among countries.

The immediate focus of the complaint is internal indeterminacy in all the most influential models of international trade. However, internal and external indeterminacy are connected. Later in this chapter I discuss the peculiar and sterilizing relation between formal analysis and causal conjecture that has come to characterize economics since the time of marginalism and that was already foreshadowed in Ricardo's thought experiment about comparative advantage as the proximate source of external indeterminacy: the facts are kept far away and only selectively approached. This relation is also the ultimate source of the internal indeterminacy.

There are any number of models that make contradictory stipulations in the hope of justifying, by different routes, the same program of free trade conducted on the basis of comparative advantage. At the same time, for the same reasons that there are so many and such contradictory models, each of them generates too many alternative answers to the question, in the production of what should a given country specialize? Or else it narrows the answers down only by making its factual stipulations ever more simplistic and unreal and its analytic implications ever less revealing.

A second objection, coming from those who would restrict the application of the doctrine of comparative advantage rather than from those who would extend it, is that under certain all too plausible assumptions, comparative advantage gives way to absolute advantage. If one factor of production (for example, capital) is mobile, rates of return to the mobile factor will be equalized across countries. Absolute advantage, in Adam Smith's old sense, then accrues to the country with the lowest costs of the immobile factors (for example, labor) incurred per production unit, as determined by the costs of the immobile factors in combination with their productivity.*

Advocates of free trade will find little comfort in this collapse; a generalized prescription of free trade that has ceased to rest on the foundation of comparative advantage cannot be reliably rebuilt on the basis of absolute advantage. It is true that under the case of absolute advantage and disadvantage that I have described, of mobile capital and immobile labor, increased trade may nevertheless expand the consumption possibilities of each trading country. It will do so, however, in the company of important and conflict-ridden distributional consequences. For example, as capital leaves a country (to reap the rewards of its mobility), labor income will fall (whether through employment or wage adjustment), and capital income will increase. (It is a result described in the technical literature as the Stolper-Samuelson effect, within the framework of the Heckscher-Ohlin model, which I later discuss. However, here this result is produced for an entirely different reason.) Conflict over the distributive consequences of such a situation is likely to overshadow the gains from trade. At the limit, the country suffering from the absolute disadvantage may suffer a calamitous loss of productive activity and capacity while its rentier class profits.

*Some have contended that absolute advantage cannot exist given certain assumptions, even the assumptions of the Heckscher-Ohlin model, which has been the most influential version of the doctrine of comparative advantage (and which is discussed in the note at the end of this chapter). They are right, but not in the sense that they mean. Their conclusion sounds as the thirteenth chime of a clock, casting doubt not only on itself but also on the previous twelve chimes and on the clock itself. Absolute advantage may be impossible in certain theories, but it is realized in fact. In many circumstances—especially in the circumstance described above, characteristic and revealing of present globalization— absolute advantage may overpower comparative advantage in significance. It has been said that an economist is someone who, on seeing that something works in practice, tries to discover if it also works in theory. Sometimes economics fails to rise to this level.

A third objection is that a vast literature on trade "in higher dimensions," that is, with more than two countries, commodities, and factors, shows that the results of the doctrine of comparative advantage—particularly those that follow from or are related to the Heckscher-Ohlin model—remain in great part robust even when applied in the complicating circumstances of the higher dimensions. We may still, for example, be able to predict uniquely the factor content of a country's trade even when we cannot predict its commodity composition. The argument from indeterminacy would, according to this objection, fail to do justice to the supposed success of established theory in meeting this test.

In fact it is striking how much the higher dimensions theorizing remains fixated on the factor composition of the product and of exports. (Ricardo's original statement of the doctrine, although less elaborate, was both deeper and more comprehensive, not least because it reached beyond the analysis of comparative static efficiencies to a theory of growth relating growth to distributive conflict.) The core issue in the argument from indeterminacy is the availability of determinate allocations of comparative advantage given certain premises. Analysis of the consequences for the average composition of output and traded goods of the relative scarcity of different factors of production is simply an aspect of this problem. What we need to know—and what received thinking fails to provide—is an adequate view of the relation between this aspect of the problem and the other aspects.

On one side are the relative scarcities of the factors. On the other side are the distinct technological and organizational capabilities of the trading partners. (The importance of national differences in the possession of these capabilities was central to Ricardo's analysis of comparative advantage. It was, however, disregarded by much of the subsequent theory of international trade, including the influential Heckscher-Ohlin model, which assumed universal access to the same pool of technologies of production.)

The decisive issue, and the one addressed by the argument from indeterminacy, is not how the relative scarcities of the factors play out in different product and export profiles, as much of the contemporary discussion seems to suppose; it is what happens when we put together the relative scarcities of the factors with the distinct technological and organizational capabilities of the trading partners, especially if we admit, as we must, that these capabilities are open to improvement and diversification.

When we perform this indispensable exercise, the difficulty of obtaining unique or even determinate solutions to the identification or assignment of comparative advantage, as a guide to specialization within the world economy, vastly increases. Instead of enlightenment about what matters most, we are left by the literature on trade in higher dimensions with ideas about what matters less. We are left with predictions of the likely factor content of an average basket of exports or products of a country, given a battery of assumptions and stipulations. We are left as well with requirements, given such stipulations and assumptions, of what the average factor content of relations among trading countries would need to be like for there to be an efficient global allocation of resources. We remain uninformed about how the acquisition of new capabilities and technologies by some countries, and the failure of others to acquire them, would modify these conclusions. As a result, we are not provided with at least half of the basis on which to predict or to propose that a particular economy develop distinctive specializations within the world economy. Without the missing half, we cannot know for sure what to make of the half with which we are presented. In this way, indeterminacy is evaded by triviality, and triviality concealed by evasion.

A fourth objection is that the argument from indeterminacy fails to do justice to the proven ability of the theory of international trade to make sense of many of the facts about the composition of trade flows. The opposite, however, is the case. Established theory has been unsuccessful in accounting for the actual content of the worldwide division of labor. Even when we consider what should be regarded as its strong suit—explaining and predicting the factor composition of the exports of different countries— the record of the tradition of ideas that developed Ricardo's doctrine of comparative advantage is notable mainly for its revealing failures.

The Leontief paradox supplies a useful wedge into the interpretation of these failures. Leontief found that, contrary to the predictions of theory, the exports of the United States were weighted toward labor-intensive products, although the American economy was relatively scarce in labor and abundant in capital. In elucidating this apparent paradox, many have remarked that its meaning is the confirmation of the thesis that greatest comparative advantage of any advanced economy lies in the ideas and capabilities that are embodied in the goods and services it produces. This source of wealth overwhelms in significance the effects of relative factor scarcities.

It is impossible to make sense of the facts about international trade without giving a major role to idea-laden skills and technologies. However, as the response to the previous objection suggested, the attempt to accommodate, following Ricardo's cue, differences of capability in our thinking about comparative advantage greatly aggravates the difficulty of arriving at unique, or even multiple but determinate, answers to the question, what specializations within the world economy should a particular country develop or maintain? The difficulties of reckoning with the facts and of thinking conclusively in theory have the same root.

In dealing with this first species of incompleteness of the doctrine of comparative advantage, we find ourselves forced to look beyond the imaginary, timeless world of static efficiency to the real, time-drenched world of transformative opportunity. The static analysis of efficiencies, with its multiple, infinite, or absent solutions, teaches us something. But how exactly we should understand the practical meaning of this teaching, when we transport it from its conceptual empyrean to our sublunary, historical existence, remains unclear. The sense of the truth that we know depends on the sense of truths that we are missing.

Incompleteness: Confusion Resulting from Uncertainty about the Limits of Our Power Collectively to Shape Comparative Advantage

Comparative advantage can be created as well as discovered; that is a proposition almost as old as the concept of comparative advantage itself. This tenet has been reinforced by some of the intellectual developments discussed in the note at the end of this chapter, including those that explore the implications for trade of the idea that there may be increasing rather than constant returns to scale in production.

When, however, we try to understand the forms and limits of the power of countries, of their firms and governments, to make or reshape comparative advantage, we soon run into trouble: problems with which our received ways of thinking about economic activity are unable adequately to deal. This trouble combines within itself a theoretical conundrum and a programmatic task. The theoretical conundrum is how to dissociate the idea that comparative advantage can be made from the idea that it can be made according to blueprint, top down. The programmatic task is how to imagine the institutions and practices by which a society can create comparative advantage.

Begin with a terminological clarification. Natural comparative advantage has often been contrasted to acquired comparative advantage. The more fundamental and useful distinction, however, is between established comparative advantage, whether or not afforded by natural circumstance, and constructed comparative advantage. This second, more basic distinction contrasts taking the present comparative advantages as given to the development of new comparative advantages: fate to will.

Consider in its most general form the problem presented by the construction of comparative advantage: who can and should serve as the agent of this construction? There are two main candidates, the market and the government. It has been conventional to treat their agency as inversely related: more power to one supposedly means less power to the other. An analogous difficulty arises in making use of either the market or the government as an agent for making new comparative advantage. The problem is the inadequacy of the present forms of economic and political life in the work of creating comparative advantage. It is necessary to experiment, and then to move forward in the light of the insight won through experimentation, rather than advance through a blueprint. However, neither the market economy nor democratic politics as they are now organized provides an adequate vehicle for the needed experimentation.

The world, you may think, is always organized to reproduce itself, not to revise itself by eliciting insight to inform change. If you think so, however, you are mistaken: the world, or any part of it, can be so organized as to have a greater or lesser bias to the perpetuation of its own arrangements and of the productive specializations that have been established on their basis.

Every real market economy is organized to distribute access to the resources and opportunities of production unequally. However, some market economies, according to the character of the economic, social, and political arrangements, distribute it much more unequally than others. Every attempt to expand access to such resources and opportunities (for example, the democratization of both agriculture and finance in nineteenth-century America) results in reconstructing some of the institutions and practices that define what the market economy is. This observation gives rise to an empirical proposition bridging the internal and external organization of economies and one that can be justified on the basis of historical example and comparative study: the less opportunity a market economy provides (the more people it either excludes altogether or includes on terms of unequal access), the more defective a device it becomes for experimentation with arrangements that sustain new comparative advantage and that justify, on the basis of such arrangements, new productive specializations within the world economy.

Every particular market order is organized in a particular way. There is a distance of uncertain length between the abstract idea of a market economy and its realization in particular institutions and arrangements. Every decisive expansion of opportunity to and through a market economy requires innovation in its institutional forms. Some institutionalized expressions of the market will be more socially inclusive than others. They will be more likely to afford to more people and more firms access to the key resources of work and production.

At this point in the argument, we come to a matter of major potential significance. Not only may market economies differ in the power to expand opportunity, they may differ as well in the extent to which they establish in the country a single version of themselves: a single regime of contract and property, a single set of rules governing production and exchange, saving and investment.

The idea that the market can assume alternative institutional forms, although acknowledged in principle, is granted so little force in either theoretical speculation or practical policy that we rarely notice one of its corollaries: if there are alternative institutional variants of a market economy, there is no reason why some such alternatives should not be allowed to coexist within the same national economy. Instead of a single property regime, for example, there could be alternative regimes of private or social property. These alternative regimes might be assigned to different sectors or scales of production, or they might, to some extent, be a matter for choice among the economic agents who would participate in them.

Such an advance toward institutional plurality is not only compatible with the idea of a market economy, it is also faithful to its animating impulse. Why should we prize the greatest possible freedom to combine factors of production while denying ourselves the power to experiment, not just in moments of crisis but all the time and in small steps, with the elements composing the institutional setting of production and exchange? There may be obstacles to the coexistence, within the same economic order, of alternative versions of the market economy. However, these practical problems are likely to have practical solutions and to influence the pace and form rather than the direction and goal of the change. The advance toward institutional plurality can be justified in part on the basis of its role in fostering productive potential, manifested in international trade as constructed comparative advantage.

Just as we cannot infer from the abstract idea of a market economy how inclusive it will be in practice, so we cannot infer from that idea the particular institutions and practices defining its content. The general equilibrium analysis that was the consummate product of the marginalist tradition in economics has obscured this truth. An economy can be "in equilibrium" with greater or lesser real access and opportunity. It can be "in equilibrium" under one or another set of institutional arrangements and legal rules.

Restraints on economic opportunity may appear in the form of "rigidities" imposing obstacles on market-clearing behavior and allowing certain favored parties to extract rents from other, disfavored ones. However, they may also (and very often will also) be invisible, hidden in presuppositions to which no one has imagined an alternative. To return to the nineteenth-century American example, the way in which the "English" path of agrarian concentration denied opportunity to family farmers, able to profit from cooperative competition with one another as well as from strategic cooperation with national and local government, did not become evident until this American alternative (or its counterparts in continental Europe) had developed. Similarly, the way in which a system of financial concentration under the control of national banks, dazzled by the prospects of profiting from easy gain from the public debt, denied financial opportunity to producers and consumers could not be clearly recognized until a far more decentralized credit system had been created. The finding of denied opportunity is retrospective rather than antecedent: it characteristically depends on the discovery of other ways of organizing economic activity and on the harsh conflicts among real interests in which this discovery is unavoidably entangled.

The market economy that is best able to exploit opportunities for the creation of comparative advantage will be—the democrat wagers, on the basis of historical experience and empirical judgment—the one that can most readily correct itself in the two related ways I have described: by giving more access to more economic agents in more ways and by freeing itself as much as possible from any single, dogmatic, entrenched expression of itself. The broadening of access will characteristically require innovation in the institutional arrangements for production and exchange. Which innovations they will require, however, is not something that can be established by general and prior formula. There is no blueprint.

Revision of the institutional framework of economic activity for the sake of broadening access and opportunity may take place, as it did in nineteenth-century American agriculture and finance, even when the superstitious confusion of the idea of a market economy with a particular, contingent set of economic arrangements continues to reign. However, the prospects for such revision will be strengthened immensely once that superstition is overthrown in practice as well as in thought.

To overthrow it in thought means to recognize that a market economy can adopt radically divergent institutional forms, including different regimes of property and contract and different ways of relating government and private producers. The forms now established in the leading economies represent the fragment of a larger and open-ended field of possibilities.

To overthrow it in practice means to organize a market economy so that it already contains different versions of itself within the same economic order, each of these versions a starting point for further institutional experiments. These different versions will include different regimes of private or social property and different combinations of private, social, and governmental initiative. The different regimes and combinations may coexist experimentally within the same national or regional market economy, whether assigned to different sectors and scales of production or chosen by the economic agents.

A market economy cannot create its own institutional presuppositions. Such presuppositions come from outside, from politics. The existing social world, with its structure of stronger and weaker interests, will work to reproduce itself. It will find an ally in prestigious superstitions, such as the belief that the market order has a single natural and necessary institutional form or that the different countries of the world converge, by evolutionary decantation, to a single set of best practices and arrangements. This struggle for self-reproduction will limit the chances for experimental innovation in the development of new market organization and new comparative advantage. The present, acting through the logic of established interests and the tools of power at their disposal, will hold the future ransom.

There are, in the end, only two directions in which this dependence of the future on the present—the path dependency of social experience—can be weakened. One is to create a hard power that seeks to lift itself over the particular interests of society. The other is to radicalize democratic experimentalism in culture as well as in politics. The first direction hits against intractable limits. No such hard power can be sustained that fails to have real ties to the real interests of society or that forgets to subordinate its experiments in policy to its stake in self-preservation.

The second direction has no limits in principle. However, it has neither a self-evident institutional content nor a foreordained social constituency. Like the concept of a market economy, the idea of democracy lacks any natural and necessary institutional form. Moreover, the radicalization of democracy is feasible only if it is shown to offer a combination of powerful interests a way to achieve what the established order denies them. The content has to be supplied by a political imagination working with the institutional materials at hand. The constituency has to be produced together with the program.

Consider the argument in retrospect. Our confusion about the nature and limits of our ability to produce and reshape comparative advantage cannot be dispelled by any set of moves within economic analysis as narrowly understood. We are forced to cross another boundary to the thinking about static efficiency within which our inherited views of comparative advantage have been formed: the false belief that the idea of a market economy has a single, natural expression. The best institutional expression of the idea, and the one that offers the most promising template for the making of comparative advantage, will be the one that affords more access to more economic agents on more terms and that least entrenches any particular species of itself, either throughout the economy or for good. No institutional formula can guarantee this result. The problem will be how to arrange things so that the formulas can be sacrificed to the goal.

Here is another way of stating the same idea. The market is the best mechanism to assign and create comparative advantage, but not any actual market, only the idea of the market. Any actual market economy is a more or less unreliable expression of the idea. It is unreliable both because it restricts opportunity and because it entrenches a limited and limiting version of the idea of a market economy. The existing market economy will never be fully self-correcting, although some versions of the market economy will have greater powers of self-correction than others. These are the versions that are most prodigal in broadening opportunity. They will also be the versions that are most pluralistic in providing within the same economic order for different variants of market order, including alternative regimes of property and contract.

These two attributes, of inclusiveness and pluralism, are likely to be associated. A decisive advance in the inclusiveness of a market economy—in its ability to offer access to more economic agents on more terms—characteristically requires innovation in its institutional forms, in just the way that the examples from nineteenth-century American history illustrate. However, the barrier will be less restrictive, and the resources for further innovation richer and less dependent on crisis and conflict, if the established arrangements already incorporate alternative institutional interpretations of a market economy.

Because no market economy creates its own institutional presuppositions or can fully correct its own failures of inclusiveness and pluralism, it is necessary to go outside the market to politics. We may then succumb to the search for a blueprint. The most aggressive version of such a blueprint will be some type of governmental direction of the economy. The blueprint, however, may also take the form of a strategy handed, top down, by the government and its bureaucratic apparatus about which comparative advantages to create. Or it may even take the form of a novel but nevertheless dogmatic conception of how a market economy should be organized. The whole problem consists in this: to question, in practice as well as in thought, the credentials of the actual market to represent the idea of the market—in particular, its credentials to serve as the setting for the construction as well as for the utilization of comparative advantage—but to do so without embracing a blueprint.

This is not merely a puzzle in theory. It is also a problem in the reimagination and the remaking of the institutional forms of both market economies and democracies. It connects the debate about comparative advantage, and about the limits to its construction, with the program of democratic experimentalism.

Thus, in addressing this second aspect of the incompleteness of comparative advantage, we must go beyond a world of static efficiency, in which markets are either perfect, and therefore reliable discoverers and creators of comparative advantage, or imperfect, and therefore needful of localized regulatory correction, to another world, in which the institutional content of both market economies and democratic politics is at issue. In that new world we find that we are not entitled to trust either the market economy or democratic politics, as they are now organized, to reveal and to produce comparative advantage.

Incompleteness: Embarrassment Resulting from the Assumption that the World Is Divided into Sovereign States

The third species of the incompleteness of the doctrine of comparative advantage is the least remarked. It is, however, both the most obvious and the one with the most subversive implications for the way we are accustomed to think about free trade.

What distinguishes the special case of trade from the general case of market-based exchange is simply the political division of humanity, and all that we associate with this division. We suppose the world to be divided into sovereign states or into other supranational or subnational entities with some of the attributes of sovereignty. What is the relation of that division to our idea of the nature and benefits of free trade? Is the division an obstacle to or an opportunity for realizing those benefits? And what is the relation between the interests and ideals inspiring the division and the ideals and interests that ought to drive the cause of free trade?

You might think that these questions would be among the first addressed in any discussion of free trade. On the contrary, they go almost unmentioned, their overpowering consequences in fact being in proportion to their near complete absence from the theoretical elaboration of comparative advantage. The setting of political division on the basis of which trade is to take place appears as an adventitious fact, what in natural science we are accustomed to label a boundary condition.

It is not a natural fact; it is a construction of our wills and imaginations. Its future lies within the collective power of mankind to change. We shall never grasp what free trade is or could become until we understand better than we do now the relation between the partition of the world into states or statelike entities and the forms of economic exchange crossing the boundaries established by this partition. We shall never make the right sense of the idea of comparative advantage until we disentangle that idea from whatever adheres to it by virtue of unreasoning and unacknowledged acceptance of the factitious political background in which trade, free or unfree, takes place.

Of all the traits we habitually associate with the present existence of states as the natural setting of trade, none stands in greater apparent tension with the impulses that are supposed to justify market-based exchange in general and free trade in particular, none exercises a more decisive influence over the circumstances of mankind today, than the limitation of the right of labor to cross national boundaries. No particular degree of restraint on the international mobility of labor is an inherent feature of the existence of states, for states, being contingent human artifacts, can have no essential attributes. Constraint on the movement of people across state boundaries is nevertheless so regularly associated with the types of states that exist today, and exercises such far-reaching effects on every aspect of social life, that the granting of a universal right to live and work abroad would radically alter both what the political divisions within humanity mean and what they cause to happen.

From the standpoint of the efficiency concerns lying at the center of our conventional beliefs about trade on the basis of established or constructed comparative advantage, as they have been narrowly and traditionally interpreted, it would be better that there be no such political divisions within mankind. Without such divisions, the chief historical basis for restraints on trade would disappear. The special category of trade would lose its identity, submerged in the general category of market-based exchange, conducted on the ground of productive specialization or a division of labor.

From the perspective of those same efficiency concerns, broadly defined to include the greatest possible freedom to deploy and recombine factors of production, all limits to the mobility of labor represent an evil. To the extent that such limits result from the existence of sovereign states, the champion of efficiency, as efficiency has been conventionally understood, would have reason to deplore the existence of such states. If, however, sovereign states can reconcile themselves to far-reaching freedom of movement for labor, their existence will be less objectionable, at least according to the traditional view of efficiency gains, achieved through market exchange and specialized production.

To say so is not to deny the formidable difficulties and the vast dangers that would attend any attempt to introduce, even by steps, a universal right of labor to cross national frontiers. It is, however, to indicate the direction of any policy that remains faithful to the professed gospel of efficiency through an enlarged freedom to trade and to combine factors of production. The direction should matter more than the length of any particular step taken in treading the path it marks out.

No sooner do we begin to recover from our surprise at the ease with which the political background of state division and immobile labor is accepted by those who have reason to oppose it than we notice that something else is missing. An interest of fundamental importance to economic activity is absent from this account of the economic significance of political division. It can be brought under the heading of a single word: diversity. The political partition of humanity provides a partial functional equivalent to the existence of distinct species as protagonists of natural evolution.

The political divisions within mankind, of which the existence of sovereign states is merely a special case, immensely expand incitements to diversity of experience, vision, organization, and action. Over the last two centuries, states have largely become the political organization of nations, or they have created nations after the fact. The most compelling justification of their separate existence is that they can represent a form of moral specialization within humanity, embodying and developing distinct forms of life and of consciousness. Humanity is so constituted, by its transcendence over all the particular structures of society and of culture it builds and inhabits, that it can develop its powers only by developing them in different directions. Distinct forms of consciousness will remain evanescent and insecure so long as they fail to be expressed in the practical arrangements of society, including its economic arrangements. Bereft of such expression, they risk being reduced to the role of folklore or escapism.

The existence of separate states—or of the other political divisions within humanity that may take their place—is a permanent inducement to diversity of economic arrangements as well as of all other institutions and practices. Political separation supports substantive difference: differences in ways of organizing work and whole economies as well as differences in the range and nature of what is produced. To the question, diversity of what?, the answer then is, diversity of every aspect of economic life, from the most basic and invisible to the most particular and tangible. The diversity encouraged by the political division of the world into separate states may include, at the most fundamental level, a greater opportunity to develop new and original institutional arrangements, including the regimes of property and contract and the relation between governmental power and private enterprise that give a market economy its distinctive shape. It may relate to ways of organizing work, developing and imparting skills, and combining people, ideas, and machines. It may therefore touch as well on the design and application of the technologies of production. At the surface of economic activity it may apply to the range of goods and services and to the composition of desires for consumption. Every one of these features of an economy may take an original turn as a result of the place it occupies within the life of a people that, by virtue of its separate existence in a separate state, can more easily develop characteristic experiences and adopt distinctive arrangements.

This boost to diversity seems too obvious to deserve mention. Astonishingly, however, the all-important relation of diversity to efficiency (efficiency narrowly understood) plays no part in classical conceptions of comparative advantage.

In thinking about trade, it is not enough to seek the most efficient uses of established or constructed comparative advantage, including those (labeled Pareto-improving) that are said to better the situation of all the trading partners. It is vital to do so within a framework of institutions and assumptions that supplies, to great and ever increasing extent, the precious raw material of diversity. Our understanding of efficiency is likely to be transformed, in theory and in practice, by its combination with this separate goal.

The partition of the world into separate states or state like entities (even if they are no more than the member states of a federal union) is—I have pointed out—the defining premise of the theory of international trade. Without it, trade would collapse into market-based exchange, and the theory applicable to the latter would apply to the former.*

Yet, paradoxically, from the perspective of a view content with traditional notions of efficiency and comparative advantage, the survival of separate states and, with them, of powerful restraints on the international mobility of labor must be regarded as an obstacle. It may be an obstacle to which we must resign ourselves, but it is an obstacle nevertheless.

*That such a collapse would occur is made explicit in the idea of "integrated world equilibrium," or IWE, associated with Paul Samuelson and then with Avinash Dixit and Victor Norman. An IWE is the equilibrium that would result if the world were a single country, with free mobility of factors of production. Under the assumptions that give rise to factor price equalization in the Heckscher-Ohlin model of comparative advantage, discussed in the note at the end of this chapter, the equalized factor rewards are the same in a world divided into separate states as in the IWE. Of course, where goods and services are produced and to nationals of which country the factor rewards accrue will depend on exactly what the political partition is and to whom ownership of the factors is assigned, that is, the "factor endowments."

The economic value of the political division within humanity lies in its contribution to all the interests that, in contrast to the criterion of static efficiency, we can put under the heading of diversity. That this division should be regarded by standard economic and trade theory as an accidental boundary condition and even as an arbitrary and costly burden (although without it all distinction between trade and market-based exchange would cease) confirms a striking infirmity of that theory: its failure to give diversity its due and to rank it as an economic goal of stature equal to efficiency, both necessary and insufficient conditions for the attainment of our higher ends. In this respect, it provides a counterpart to the most influential forms of contemporary (Anglo-American) liberal philosophy, with their insistence on treating diversity as what we want to master rather than, as Mill, Tocqueville, Herzen, and Humboldt held, what we want to produce.

What would an economic theory look like that treated the deepening of diversity, including diversity of the institutional arrangements defining a market economy, as an intermediate goal equal in importance to the achievement of efficient resource allocation on the basis of established institutional arrangements? Such a theory might deviate in method, character, and direction from many established tenets of economics. There is no better way to foreshadow its work than to rethink the doctrine of free trade, conducted on the basis of established or constructed comparative advantage.

The existence of separate states or statelike entities has ordinarily been accompanied by the imposition of forceful restraints on the movement of labor across national frontiers. However, the association between the political partition of the globe and the imprisonment of labor within the separate territories of the partition is contingent and revisable. Much more freedom of movement than now exists could in fact be reconciled, and in the earlier nineteenth-century episode of globalization was in fact reconciled, with the reality and the principle of the partition.

The simple logic of maximum liberty to combine factors of production suggests the greatest possible freedom, prudently achieved by steps, for labor to work at will anywhere in the world.

The salient qualification is that the flow of people must not be so massive, so sudden, and so unbalanced by compensating initiatives that it threaten to trigger popular and political reactions dangerous to the diversity of states and to the distinct forms of life, consciousness, and organization that flourish within their boundaries.

By the same token, political division will be less likely to support diversity of experience and of experiment if the power of the separate entities of the world to deviate and to rebel is diminished. That power may be compromised indirectly by international economic regimes, like the nineteenth-century gold standard or its contemporary functional equivalent (the strategy of acquiescing in low levels of domestic saving and weak links between saving and production as well of depending on foreign capital and of letting it come and go freely) that tie the hands of national governments and give financial markets the power to veto their would-be heresies and adventures. It may also be weakened directly by the political and economic subjection of one state to another.

When David Ricardo offered his famous example of cloth and wine, England and Portugal, Portugal was little more than a protectorate of Britain. The Portuguese wine trade was increasingly to come under English ownership; its power to serve as a stepping stone to other lines of production and trade was limited by its assigned place in the economic designs of foreigners. Yet there was no room in the truncated doctrine of comparative advantage for such an observation because there was no opportunity in the mode of thought of which that doctrine formed a part to consider the requirements of efficiency and diversity in relation to each other.

Suppose that humanity were not so divided; that there were a world state, not admitting of any substantial political divisions within itself, not even those characteristic of a federal or confederal union; and that the concept of trade therefore ceased to have any meaning distinct from the general meaning of market exchange among specialized producers. The burden of creating diversity could no longer fall, as it has so heavily fallen, on the separate sovereign states of the world. It would have to be supported by the same universal order, through its internal impulse to deepen difference, especially difference of legal regime and economic organization, within itself.

There would be all the more reason to favor an economic order allowing different legal realizations of the idea of a market economy, including different regimes of private and social property and contract, to coexist experimentally—for example, in different sectors of the economy or at different scales of production. Diversification, from having been delegated to distinct political entities, would have to be made internal, as indeed it should be for the sake of our emancipation as well of our enrichment, so long as separate states continue to exist.

In addressing this third species of incompleteness of the doctrine of comparative advantage, we move beyond static efficiency to deal with the creation and diversification of the stuff on which comparative advantage can do its selective work. If we have, in the form of the doctrine of comparative advantage, the theory of selective work without the theory of the diversification of the material, we have only half of the theory that we need. Once again, we find that we cannot address the problem of the allocation of tasks across economies without confronting that of the multiplication of possibilities within them. We dare not be confident of knowing the meaning of the part we think we master, until we come into possession of the part we miss. By a remarkable paradox, the political division of humanity is both the premise of trade theory and a fact to whose significance, transmutations, and possible functional equivalents—from the standpoint of the interest in diversity of stuff—the theory is, and has always been, blind.

Beyond Incompleteness: The Sham Similarity between Postmarginalist Economics and Physics

The theory of comparative advantage, still the centerpiece of established thinking about free trade, is and remains radically incomplete in each of the three ways I have described. The point is not just that something vital is missing that turns out to be indispensable to policy as well as to understanding. The point is that we cannot know the theoretical and practical value of the part we have until we combine it with the part we lack. The established practice of economic analysis is not only unable to provide the missing part, it is also incapable of grasping the nature and implications of the incompleteness.

One way to advance in understanding the implications of this situation is to compare economics as it has taken shape in the tradition begun by nineteenth-century marginalism with physics, and especially to compare the relation between causal explanation and mathematical representation in each of them. The relation is fundamentally different, and the difference sheds light on the incompleteness of the doctrine of comparative advantage (as well as of established economic ideas in general) and on the way to overcome it.

As the hardest of the social sciences and the one that has established the most intimate association with mathematics, economics seems to follow in the footsteps of physics. And so it has been seen by many of its leading practitioners. Schumpeter remarked that the marginalist revolution could be compared with Newton's revolution only in the sense that the Haitian revolution could be compared with the French. However, in flaunting the European prejudice, he was accepting the claim of economics to resemble physics while depreciating the magnitude of the intellectual innovations that marginalism had produced.

Newton had intuited the substance of his laws of motion before he had found in the calculus that he (and Leibniz) invented the great mathematical instrument in which to express them, with its characteristic power to generate dynamical equations suited to the representation of change within time. The partnership of the physical intuition with the mathematical expression turned out to be exemplary as well as seminal in the history of the alliance between science and mathematics. It also drew attention to an enigma that has continued to haunt that alliance.

The "unreasonable effectiveness of mathematics" for physics is nowhere more disconcerting than in the bond it implies between something outside time and something within it. The relation between a cause and its effect takes place in time; the cause precedes the effect. If time were unreal, causation would be illusory as well. The relation between a mathematical or logic premise and its conclusion, however, lies outside time, although it is within time and through time-bound processes of reasoning that we reason about this relation, undergoing it as a mental event. This timeless character of mathematical or logical propositions—the senselessness of saying that they are time-bound—holds even when the mathematics describes, as the calculus does, changes that must be time-drenched if they are to be real.

The use of mathematics in this scientific tradition looks out from the internal operations of thought to the riddles of nature. Mathematical ideas may be invented after the fact to expound and develop a physical intuition about the workings of nature (as in the example of Newton's laws of motion) or they may help suggest a physical intuition yet unformed (as in the instance of contemporary string theory). In either situation, however, the subject matter remains some part of the natural world: capable of defying our causal conjectures and of outreaching the mathematical instruments by which we are able to formulate and develop them.

Newton provided science with the supreme model of a deterministic physics, a system of connected causal propositions exhaustively determining all events under their sway and fully expressed in the equations in which it was stated. Yet one should consider what happened when Poincaré had to confront, over the course of the 1890s, the conundrum in Newton's celestial mechanics that came to be known as the three-body problem. A large and a small planet gravitate around a star. The big planet is big enough to remain insensitive to the gravitational force of the small one. According to the laws established by Kepler and Newton, the large planet will move around the star in predictable elliptical orbit. However, under this seemingly modest degree of complication, we are unable, with the aid of Newton's laws of motion, to predict the movement of the small planet.

At first the problem may seem analogous to the difficulties arising for the theory of comparative advantage when we complicate Ricardo's example of wine and cloth, Portugal and England, to take account of more than two commodities and more than two countries. Depending on our stipulations about these more complicated circumstances, and our judgments about what constitutes a solution, there may be multiple solutions for the assignment of comparative advantage, or infinite solutions, or no solutions. The subsequent history of the three-body problem, however, shows just how deep-cutting is the difference between the dominant explanatory practices in physics and in economics.

Mittag-Leffler's discovery of an error in Poincaré's proof of a supposed solution to the three-body problem within the limits of Newtonian physics eventually prompted Poincaré to develop the ideas published, between 1892 and 1899, as "New Methods of Celestial Mechanics." Poincaré had to grasp the more complicated situation as a "nonintegrable system," for the analysis of which Newton's differential equations turned out to inadequate. To understand the long-term behavior of such a system, he chose to focus on the few of its motions that were periodic, seizing on them as the "only opening" by which to enter the "hitherto inaccessible fortress" of its nonperiodic motions. In the end, he had to inaugurate a wholly new branch of mathematics, chaos theory, suitable to the mathematical representation and analysis of systems hypersensitive to even modest changes in their initial conditions. The resulting ideas did not deny the possibility of calculating the motions of the third body in the three-body problem, so long as one could rely on enough computational power to work through the consequences of different initial conditions. However, they exemplified a form of statistical or probabilistic determination that was alien both to Newton's physics and to his mathematics.

That this event was characteristic rather than atypical of the history of modern physics can be shown by its similarities to Mikhail Gromov's discovery almost a hundred years later, in 1980, of an uncertainty result or principle in classical mechanics having to do with the difficulty, within the systems Gromov studied, of either creating or transferring information. Once again, it was mysterious nature that knocked at the door. Once again, an intuition about the workings of nature had to be developed through mathematical innovations (related, in this instance, to the geometry of "hypersurfaces").

The history of theorizing about comparative advantage offers—and, within the boundaries of the analytic tradition of which it later became a part, it can offer—no true parallel to this remarkable dialectic of empirical study, causal conjecture, and mathematical discovery. The contrasting mathematical expressions provide a clue to the source of the problem. The equations of comparative advantage for which we hope to find solutions are devoted to the service of a static comparative analysis; they contain no true dynamics. Ricardo's initial conclusions followed by inexorable logic from the stipulations of his example, although their charm lay in reaching by these means conclusions that were felt to be counterintuitive. The stark simplifications on which his thought experiment drew were analogous in character to the simplifications of later theories although different in content from them. (Of these theories, the most influential, the Heckscher-Ohlin model, is discussed in a note at the end of this chapter.) The subsequent trajectory of economics from marginalism on to general-equilibrium analysis confirmed this analytic practice, fixing its personality and giving it a program.

Newton's image of the workings of nature looked outward to the real world of time and causation, proposing a view that no triumph of logic could have derived from a set of premises. Ricardo's thought experiment looked inward, using pure logic to reveal the surprising implications of a few stipulated facts. The experiment was motivated by the hope, ever since nourished by economics, that the imaginary world of the stipulations would help us understand better the real world of causal processes. Newton's laws of motion required a mathematics capable of describing the movement of entire dynamical systems in time. Ricardo's idea of comparative advantage needed no more than a formalism suited to discovering logical implication, the better to serve a comparative static analysis. (There is, however, reason to think that Ricardo, unlike the theorists of comparative advantage who came to stand on his shoulders, used his thought experiment about England and Portugal, as he had his campaign against the corn laws, to serve a theory of growth more than an analysis of static efficiencies. The theory of growth implicit in his reasoning has been seen, in the spirit of Sraffa, as invoking the effects of free trade on the balance of income between savers, for example, owners of industry, putative agents of growth, and nonsavers, for example, landlords and workers, sacrificial victims to the impersonal requirements of economic development. For the would-be scientists of trade "in higher dimensions," no justification could be more embarrassing.) Newton's orientation outward made it inevitable that, once his physics and his mathematics were found to be incapable of accommodating the three-body problem, a novel set of physical and mathematical ideas would have to be developed to accommodate them. The outcome was Poincaré's "new laws of celestial mechanics" and his mathematical theory of chaos, and the substitution of one type of causal determination for another. Ricardo's thought experiment was meant from the outset to be incomplete, making violently simplifying assumptions intended to shed light sideways on an unaccountably messy world. No particular discovery of incompleteness (such as the forms of incompleteness discussed in the preceding pages) would be certain to disturb its conclusions, for it would remain unclear whether the incompleteness was the problem or the point. There could be no Poincaré for such Newtons.

Instead, with the rise of marginalist economics, the distinction between these two intellectual orientations became more self-conscious and more radical. From having been an occasional device, Ricardo's strategy began to seem like the proper fate of economics: the way in which economics could best become a serious science. In retrospect, the doctrine of comparative advantage turned out to be the most characteristic teaching of economics in method as well as in substance. The larger intellectual stake in this contrast of ways of relating causal explanation to mathematical analysis at last became clear.

Condemned to Eternal Infancy: Implications of the Method Inaugurated by Marginalism

The tradition of economic analysis pioneered in the late nineteenth century by Walras, Jevons, and Menger, their contemporaries, and their students is conventionally labeled marginalism. The supreme intellectual achievement to which it later gave rise was the theory of general equilibrium. I now focus on an aspect of this limited but fateful reorientation that is crucial to understanding the character of the economics that grew out of it. It is therefore also of vital importance to anyone who seeks to understand and to overcome the characteristic incompleteness of the explanations that this style of economics offers, as exemplified by the three species of incompleteness of the doctrine of comparative advantage. A continuing theme in this book is the impossibility of attaining deeper insight into the problems of trade and of the global division of labor, and of dispelling the superstitions that burden the doctrine of free trade, within the constraints of this tradition of economic ideas.

The classical English political economists, from Adam Smith to Thomas Malthus, had developed ways of thinking about economic life that combined logical analysis, causal explanation, and normative argument. Notwithstanding the restrictive character of his analysis of comparative advantage and of the thought experiments through which he formulated it, David Ricardo himself had contributed to this tradition. It was an intellectual practice rich in claims about the causes and effects of different economic phenomena. It did not borrow these claims from any other discipline; it advanced them on its own motion and to its own risk. By the same token, it did not hesitate, in the work of Smith, to associate its causal science with a vision of unrealized collective possibility, grounded in a view of human nature and of its development in history.

Karl Marx and others attacked this tradition. The keynote of Marx's attack was his thesis that the English economists had presented as universal and timeless laws of economic life what were in fact merely the regularities of a particular, time-bound economic order, "capitalism."* This impulse toward false universali-

---

*I use the terms "capitalism" and "capitalist economy" in this book as a handy, conventional reference to the particular form of a market economy that took hold in the North Atlantic countries over the last few centuries and that has since become the exemplary form of such an economy in the eyes of much of the world. The advocates of these eco-

zation of the particular and of the transitory resulted not only in a lack of imagination about alternative possibilities and transformative opportunity, it also misrepresented the workings of the capitalist order.

Marx subsumed many of the ideas of classical economics, including Ricardo's labor theory of value, under a larger historical narrative, designed both to explain capitalism and to reveal the mechanism by which it was bound to be changed and replaced. One of the many ways in which Marx resembled the economists he criticized was in his bold commitment to offering causal explanations. The interpretations of historical experience informing these causal claims as well as the claims themselves lay at the heart of his argument in *Capital*.

His system of causal propositions focused on a deep structure of formative arrangements and assumptions shaping the routine practices of exchange and production, of work and life, that took place on the basis they provided. This distinction between the hidden formative structure and the visible formed routines was a conception he shared with many other influential social theorists of nineteenth-century Europe. For him as for them, a system of causal explanation forged on the anvil of a distinction between the depth and the surface was accompanied by a series of connected necessitarian assumptions.

---

nomic institutions have often agreed with Karl Marx and his followers in representing them as a more or less indivisible system, with a predetermined content and detailed requirements. Those who profess disbelief in the assumptions of such a view continue to use the term in a way that suggests failure to grasp the implications of their own disbelief. As a result, the idea of capitalism has fallen into a degree of confusion from which it no longer seems worthwhile or even feasible to rescue it. See the discussion, under the heading "the troubles of the concept of capitalism," in my book *Social Theory: Its Situation and Its Task*, Verso, 2004, pp. 101–109. Here, I make use of the word to refer to a predominant but contingent way of organizing market-based exchange. It is the very way of organizing such exchange that the emerging world trade regime threatens to help impose on humanity as the universal background to an open international economy.

The first such assumption, of indivisibility, was that each economic and social system—Marx's mode of production—was an indivisible system: all of its parts would stand or fall together. The second assumption, of closure, was that humanity was confined to a short list of indivisible institutional alternatives, moving through the list according to a foreordained evolutionary succession. The third assumption, of lawlike progression, was that lawlike forces ruled over this advance. The attempt to rescue the central insight into the discontinuity of formative institutional and ideological contexts, underlying the routines of conflict, production, and belief, from the necessitarian baggage of these assumptions has to this day not been fully accomplished in the work of the social sciences and humanities.

Marx's criticism and his construction formed part of a wide-ranging struggle in nineteenth-century thought. In this struggle, Marx offered a wealth of causal explanations while dispensing with explicitly prescriptive proposals. What need was there of a program when history had one in store for humanity? Others preferred to attack the established tradition of political economy on avowedly normative grounds.

The response of the analytic tradition inaugurated by Walras, Menger, and Jevons to this conflict was remarkable. It has no parallel in the history of modern thought (save for Hans Kelsen's "pure theory of law" and other rigorous forms of twentieth-century legal positivism), although the fears and ambitions that help explain it have set their mark on countless episodes in the history of ideas.

Instead of joining as partisans the causal and normative fray and of continuing, in this respect, the tradition of the classical English political economists, the marginalists contrived to establish an analytic practice that would purify itself as much as possible of all controversial causal and normative claims. It would be pure analysis. It would soar above the field of battle, bringing light without heat. Its explanatory uses would rely on the combination of its analytic moves with descriptive stipulations and causal conjectures supplied from outside the analytic apparatus, by other disciplines and methods. Its policy and prescriptive uses would depend on normative points of departure, externally provided by reason, ideology, or faith. Everything controversial, whether as causal account or as normative commitment, would be treated as exogenous. The combination of the analysis with the external stipulations would in every instance account for the explanatory or programmatic results.

Noli me tangere was the watchword, and immunity the promise. The principle was analytic power without explanatory or programmatic liability. A side benefit of extraordinary importance was to turn the pure practice of economic analysis into a branch of logic and therefore to prepare it for its marriage with mathematics. The spirit prefigured in Ricardo's thought experiment about comparative advantage (although not in many other parts of his thought) had thus been rendered explicit and general.

At no moment has economics ever been completely dominated by this orientation. When marginalism first appeared, German historical and American institutional economics offered a very different intellectual practice. The seeming inability of these intellectual alternatives to generate distinctive and powerful claims and to provide a basis for a different connection between causal conjecture and mathematical analysis compromised their authority. Today, new versions of institutional and behavioral economics look to such claims and to such a connection. All along the way, from then to now, the retreat into a citadel of immunity, with its characteristic separation of analysis from explanation and prescription, has existed in an intellectual climate to which this procedure remained alien. No wonder contrasting ways of relating analysis to explanation and prescription have always penetrated the way economics is done.

Nevertheless, it would be a mistake to suppose that my criticism is directed against either the professional culture of economics (as distinguished from its characteristic methods, assumptions, and proposals) or its marriage to mathematics. It is addressed instead to the most distinctive element within the dominant tradition of economic thinking for the last hundred years, the element distinguishing this intellectual practice from all others and accounting for both its power and its limitations.

Under the aegis of this intellectual practice, economics has never ceased to move among three strategies, sometimes implemented by different economists and sometimes present in the work of the same economists. The oscillation has served to uphold the basic analytic orientation while both obfuscating its nature and mitigating its costs.

The strategy of purism is to insist on the full rigor of the distinction between the analytic operations of economics and the empirical or prescriptive starting points that must be supplied to it from outside. The empirical in turn includes both descriptive stipulation and causal explanation. Restrained within this rigor, economic analysis can explain or prescribe only through the borrowed power of such external provisions. It is powerful to amplify but impotent to penetrate. It shines with reflected light. In its analytical core, it is as innocent as Pontius Pilate.

This is the version of economics that we see most insistently practiced by general equilibrium theorists like Gerard Debreu. Taken to the hilt, its result is to turn economics into the logical tool of alien knowledge, argument, or commitment. The particular cognitive by-products of this intellectual activity will be findings of constraint and clarifications of trade-offs, inferred, by force of analysis, from someone else's stipulations. Tell me the facts about society and about your preferences, and I shall make you think clearly and face the implications of your own suppositions, says the hard-headed analyst.

The strategy of pretension sacrifices purism for the sake of programmatic potency. However, it rarely acknowledges this sacrifice. It is economics as a partisan in the ideological and institutional disputes of the contemporary world. It characteristically urges the benefits of markets, of capitalism, of globalization, and above all of free trade. The excellences of free trade, conducted on the basis of comparative advantage, has been its most characteristic if not its most general teaching. Relying on these doctrines, it does not hesitate to make a host of particular policy recommendations. It is exemplified by the overtly programmatic arguments of economists from Ludwig von Mises to Milton Friedman.

Two controversial intellectual linkages are crucial to the strategy of pretension. The first linkage, widely discussed and relatively less important, is the identification of a model of maximizing, self-interested behavior, of the principle of marginal utility, and of the concept of allocational efficiency with the workings of a market economy: the market economy as the superior, even as the natural and necessary, institutional vehicle of those ideas and orientations. This association was the subject matter of the controversy in the 1930s about the reconciliation of marginalist economics with state planning in which Oskar Lange and other socialist economists played a major part. The outcome was to demonstrate that there was no strictly analytical obstacle to the deployment of marginalist concepts and techniques by state planners. The practical costs of *dirigisme* might be formidable and even overwhelming, but they could not be deduced from the analysis of marginal utility, maximizing behavior, and static efficiency. Argument about them had to go forward on a different plane, sunk in disputes about what caused what in present-day economies and what alternatives to present arrangements were feasible and accessible.

The second linkage, much less remarked and far more significant, is the identification of the abstract idea of a market economy with a particular, historically contingent set of economic institutions and practices, including a particular regime of property and contract. The point is to represent these arrangements as the constant and inseparable expression of the great ideas standing behind them. Bereft of detailed institutional content, the abstractions are insufficient to support policy prescriptions and criticisms. Equipped with such content, they mark a distinctive path in the ideological conflicts of the day; they allow the particular to speak with the authority of the general.

It was and is an impulse premised on disregard for a truth with which economics to this day has failed fully to reckon: that the detailed legal and institutional content of a market economy cannot be inferred from the concept of such an economy any more than the detailed legal and institutional content of democracy can be inferred from the idea of democracy; that market economies may be organized in ways very different from those that have come to prevail in the recent history of the North Atlantic societies; that the potential for difference extends to rules and arrangements for property and contract as well as to the relations between economic agents and the state; and that these large and forceful differences cannot be judged except by those who are willing to enter the open field of controversy about social reality and possibility in which the ideas of maximizing behavior and marginal utility have, unless further accompanied and equipped, little or nothing to say.

The strategy of equivocation departs from purism in the interest of explanatory force and of the power to recommend policy that such force may support. It incurs, but only half-heartedly and with mental reservation, the fault of which Marx accused the English political economists: the unwarranted generalization of the local and the transitory. It seeks to establish regularities among lawlike macroeconomic aggregates such as the levels of savings, investment, and employment. Under challenge, it acknowledges that these regularities depend for their force on a host of particular institutional arrangements far more detailed and distinctive than those defining our general idea of capitalism or the market economy—for example, the precise way in which labor is organized and empowered in its dealings with capital, or the scope of unemployment insurance, or the powers enjoyed by the central bank. Were any of these many loosely connected background facts to change, they concede, so would the supposed regularities. Thus, they decline to make in strong form the universalizing claim that laid the English political economists open to Marx's attack: the confusion of the "laws" of all economies with the "laws" of a particular economy.

So long, however, as a society lies in the grip of relative institutional and ideological stagnation, so long as its formative arrangements and beliefs come under little effective challenge, so long as the trauma of war or ruin fails to jeopardize what the disarmed imagination leaves untouched, the concession of principle can be disregarded in the practice of argument. The relations among large-scale economic phenomena, shaped against this relatively quiescent background, will then take on a mendacious semblance of lawlike regularity.

If the concession that the relation between, say, inflation and unemployment depends on the particulars of the institutional and ideological context were made in earnest, the subject of inquiry would be the relation of those phenomena to this context, the nature of this context, and its prospects of transformation, rather than the relations among the phenomena against their stable and shadowy background. However, the concession is not for real. It is a ploy, denying in practice what it admits in principle.

Such was the strategy pursued, for example, by the American followers of Keynes, who, in the second half of the twentieth century, developed a "macroeconomics." They turned a theory of permanent disequilibrium into a theory of rigidities either preventing equilibrium or allowing for multiple equilibriums at higher and lower levels of employment. They made Keynes politically palatable by depoliticizing him, and formulated an agenda that took the mid-twentieth-century institutional and ideological settlement as the natural template of a modern regulated market economy. Their method of equivocating with the relation between economic phenomena and their institutional and ideological setting was then taken over by others antipathetic to the teachings of the master.

The internal life of the central tradition of economics has been a perpetual alternation between the strategy of purism on the one hand and the strategies of pretension and equivocation on the other hand. The impure explanatory and prescriptive power of the second and third strategies compensates for the radical inhibitions of the first. When pretension and equivocation are challenged for their compromises, it is always possible to retreat into purism.

The implications for any attempt to redress the three species of incompleteness in the doctrine of comparative advantage are unmistakable. We cannot redress them within the boundaries of a style of economic analysis insisting on such a separation of analysis from explanation and prescription. Now we can see why the thesis that the argument about free trade developed in this book can be fully accommodated within this style of analysis, although true in letter (if one has in mind the purest, most self-denying practice of economic analysis), is false in spirit. To address the three forms of incompleteness is, inevitably, to struggle with the intellectual practice that produces them.

The consequences of this way of relating analysis to causality and policy have been decisive for economics. They have allowed it to claim a rigor unparalleled among the social sciences but acquired at fatal cost. The cost has been to condemn economics—at least the versions of economics remaining under the sway of these ideas—to eternal infancy. The votaries of this science were mistaken to see analytic immunity to causal and normative controversy as a benefit. They committed a sin for which in thought, as in life, there is no forgiveness: they failed to cast down their shields.

A Note Relating Ideas in this Book to the Dominant Tradition of Thinking about Comparative Advantage

The history of the doctrine of comparative advantage can be presented schematically as a story in three chapters. The addition of the missing, fourth chapter reveals the hidden meaning of the previous three. I now submit this story to radical compression and nonformal, intuitive exposition, disengaging the main narrative line from all technical complication, the better to help us combine the insight provided by the standard analysis of comparative advantages with insights that this analysis denies us.

The first stage is Ricardo (stated in 1817), with its prehistory in intuitive ideas about absolute advantage, as in Adam Smith. Ricardo took account of a single factor of production, labor. He allowed for technological differences between countries and, on that basis, for differences in the productivity of their labor forces. Without such differences in technology and productivity, the case for free trade in his analysis would collapse. Autarky would prevail.

The second stage is the Heckscher-Ohlin model (first presented in 1933) and all its many sequels in subsequent economic analysis. This model made do without the differences in technology that were central to Ricardo's argument. Instead, it appealed to inequalities in capital endowments, thus reestablishing on another basis national differences in the productivity of labor. For Ricardo, these differences had, like technology itself, been exogenous. They now became endogenous to the model.

Differences in national capital endowments (for example, in investment in infrastructure) require different factor proportions. The right factor proportions for each national setting are established through the profit-maximizing decisions of the capitalist. The picture is that of a system of world trade organized along the axis of trade between capital-abundant and labor-abundant countries.

A central prediction, in manifest conflict with experience, is factor-price equalization: factor prices will converge, thanks to free trade, with traded goods prices. Among the many assumptions, all of them indispensable to the argument, are constant returns to scale and immobility of capital as well as of labor among countries (but their complete mobility within them). If capital were mobile, forming a single worldwide pool for investment, the labor-capital ratio would soon be the same all over the globe. Differences in the relative abundance of labor would no longer result in the imbalances of productivity vital to the argument. Trade in goods would collapse, and autarky predominate, as they would in Ricardo's world if countries had the same technological capabilities. In this way of thinking, different countries do have those same capabilities: the "production functions," defining the conversion of inputs into outputs, are identical and homogeneous throughout the world.

Within this realm of ideas, trade in goods can produce the effects of movement of capital and people. Factor price equalization is simply the expression of this fundamental equivalence. We can credit failure to achieve this result to some localized rigidity in markets or to a particular deviation from the assumptions defining the model without jeopardy to the central insight or to its use in understanding an unruly world, bound to transgress some of its strictures.

Many of the most influential ideas in trade theory are best understood as elaborations of this way of thinking. Thus, the Rybczynski theorem translates the static language of the Heckscher-Ohlin model into faintly dynamic idiom, without, however, suggesting even the beginnings of a standard of choice among multiple solutions to the problem of productive specialization based on comparative advantage: a shift in relative factor endowments will result in a change in the relative prominence of labor-intensive and capital-intensive production. According to the Stolper-Samuelson result, relative changes in the prices of goods will cause changes in the prices of the factors used to produce them. If the price of capital-intensive goods increases relative to the price of labor-intensive goods, the rental rate of capital will increase relative to the wage, the return to labor.

The third and last completed stage of the story develops out of the attempt to relax the assumption of constant returns to scale. By allowing for increasing returns to scale, for the possibility of achieving a "critical mass" in particular sectors and a combination of skills and efficiencies at which a set of national firms can then not easily be bested, we not only draw closer to actual experience; we also show why trade fails to collapse into autarky, as implied by Ricardo (if technological capabilities were diffused and shared) or by Heckscher-Ohlin (if capital were mobile among countries or if any other number of highly restrictive and seemingly counterfactual assumptions failed to hold). Here is the line of analysis that goes from the "strategic trade theory" of the 1970s and 1980s to more recent writings.* By acquiring entrenched niches in the global division of labor, trading countries—or, more precisely, the network of firms acting under their aegis—are able to entrench their specializations, not forever or against anything but for a while and against emerging efforts to do what they do better and more cheaply somewhere else.

However, the same argument showing why autarky need not and will not return also suggests that the gains of trade may not, in every circumstance, be universally shared. Not only firms but whole sectors of production, segments of workers, and even entire

*See, for example, Ralph E. Gomory and William J. Baumol, *Global Trade and Conflicting National Interests*, MIT Press, 2000.

national economies and their populations may stand to lose. Moreover, we may be unable to infer the choice of which strategic path to entrench, and of how best to open up such a path, from the static analysis of comparative advantage. At issue is the construction of comparative advantage. Firms, sectors, and governments may find themselves compelled to guess and to gamble about the direction to take. The price signals transmitted by the markets are neither determinate nor reliable enough to answer the questions of direction and method, for each of the real markets bears the mark of cumulative and conflicting attempts to construct comparative advantage rather than merely to reveal it.

The corrosive effect of this analysis on the classic teaching of free trade is muffled by the twin fears of dogmatism and favoritism: the anxiety that those who would strategize and select will be the knowing servants of factional interest, determined to convert public power to private advantage, when they are not the unwitting victims of prejudice and dogma. Free trade, robbed of some of its exaggerated claims and unkeepable promises, will now reappear as the instrument of experimentalism and equality against voluntarism and pillage.

The fourth chapter of this story remains largely unwritten. However, we must anticipate its content if we are to understand more fully the meaning of the three earlier chapters. A simple way to understand its main point is to say that it consists in the combination of two moves.

The first move is to maintain the full force of the idea presented in the third chapter of the story—that increasing returns to scale, as well as other supports to the entrenchment of comparative advantage, may prevent gains from trade from being universally or equally shared by the trading partners. We shall now not allow the lesson of this turn in the plot to be dulled by despair about the ability to exercise selective and strategic judgment without seeing it perverted into an instrument of dogmatism and favoritism. Instead of retreating, we shall advance. We shall acknowledge that democracy, like the market economy itself, can take alternative institutional forms and that the forms now established in the rich North Atlantic countries represent a subset of a far larger, open set of institutional possibilities. And we shall explore the conjecture that some of these forms may be less susceptible to the evils of dogma and favor than others, thus allowing the strategic and selective judgments that may seem best in principle to become best as well in practice. Everything will depend on the actual organization of the market economy and of democratic politics as two connected sets of practices of collective experimentalism, including experimentalism about the rules, institutions, and practices that shape the market economy.

The second move is to reintroduce, in more complicated, inclusive, and disturbing form, a major element of the first chapter of the story: Ricardo's assumption, indispensable within his analysis to the avoidance of autarky, of the differences between the productivity of labor that result from the distinct and unequal technologies of production available to the trading partners.

Let us now take Ricardo's assumption of different national productivities of labor based on different technological capabilities as a proxy for the different ways of organizing work among people and for combining people with machines. Let us deny that labor is homogeneous: the different forms of cooperation in a division of labor are the central and fateful part of any scheme of economic organization. Let us treat Adam Smith's pin factory model of the division of labor, with its premium on specialization and hierarchy, as the limiting case of a broader spectrum of possibilities. Let us view labor and technology as if they were different aspects of the same thing: in one instance the social and in the other the physical expression of our imaginative activity. Let us recognize that of all distinctions among types of labor, the one that is laden with the greatest consequence is the distinction between the activities that do not yet lend themselves to formulaic repetition and the activities that we have already learned how to repeat, and therefore as well how to express in formulas and embody in machines. Let us recognize that a major element in the economic ascent of modern societies lies in the capacity, conditioned by the particular organization of work, of the economy, of politics, and of culture, of using machines and the repeatable to free our time for the not yet repeatable. And let us appreciate how different ways of organizing markets and trade—ways that cannot be tellingly described or understood in the language of simple contrasts between free trade and protection—may either hinder or help this ascent.

From the ideas making up this second move, listed in the preceding paragraph, there results, in combination with my earlier argument about the incompleteness of the doctrine of comparative advantage, the way of thinking about trade that this book develops.

It is useful to look back at the story I have told with its three written chapters, followed by its fourth, imagined chapter. Two features of this story deserve the closest attention; they have fundamental relevance to an understanding of the intellectual background from which the argument of this book arises and against which it is directed.

The first feature is the central paradox in the historical development of ideas about comparative advantage and free trade. The case for free trade has often relied on assumptions that are so restrictive—and in such manifest conflict with past and present experience—that they make the impulse toward free trade seem all but miraculous. What should prevail, according to these ideas, given the failure of the restrictive assumptions, is autarky.

On the other hand, the ideas, such as increasing returns to scale, that explain why the reversion to autarky fails to occur despite the failure of the restrictive assumptions suggest that trade is more likely to be a terrain for winners and losers, among nations and classes as well as among firms, than for universal gains. The vindication of the possibility of trade comes together with the revelation of its contentiousness.

However, the meaning of this contentiousness starts to change when we begin to understand that we need not be limited to choosing between more trade or less trade or to shifting, in one direction or another, the balance between free trade and restraint on trade. We can reimagine and reorganize the trade regime, globally or regionally. We can reimagine and reorganize the market economy itself.

A second feature of the story is the star role that it properly attributes to the productivity of labor and to the return to labor (that is to say, the wage rate) in explaining the character and history of the world trading system. Nothing less is at stake than the range of our productive powers considered in relation to the organization of society. Study of the differential productivity and reward of labor provides us with a wedge into this larger concern.

To acknowledge certain facts despite the prejudices of theory and ideology that prevent them from being seen for what they are is the beginning of insight into these matters. These facts are not only of immense interest in themselves, they also reveal the limitations of the traditions of thought that have so completely failed to make sense of them.

One such fact is that the reality of world trade is not now, if it ever was, captured by the image of labor-abundant countries trading with capital-rich countries, the cheaper labor of the former complementing, through the alchemy of productive specialization on the ground of comparative advantage, the higher productivity of the latter. This is the image at the center of the Heckscher-Ohlin model and its variations, and one that is already foreshadowed in Ricardo's founding argument and his example of trade between Portugal and England. It is an almost direct translation into the reality of trade of the most elementary model of the national economy as theorized by the English political economists and reinterpreted by Karl Marx: the legally free but economically dependent worker sells his labor to the capitalist for a wage.

Reality has departed from this image in several connected ways. The most advanced forms of production are established in advanced sectors of production or vanguards in the major developing economies as well as in the rich countries. The network of such vanguards, I later argue, has become the commanding force in the world economy, exchanging ideas, practices, and people, as well as goods and services and often only weakly linked to the remainder of their own national economies, rich or poor. The essence of this productive vanguardism is not abundance of capital or even of technology; it is a set of revolutionary practices changing the character of the division of labor (farther and farther away from Adam Smith's pin factory), making good firms more closely resemble good schools, and allowing production to share in the methods and spirit of science as well as in its discoveries.

Abundant and cheaper labor may be associated with either lower or higher productivity. When labor is relatively cheap and productivity relatively high, unit-labor costs—the average labor compensation per unit of output, measuring both productivity and the cost of labor—may fall. At the end of the twentieth century and the beginning of the twenty-first, the organized and advanced sectors of the Chinese and Indian economies benefited from this situation. Relatively cheaper labor may, however, also be connected with low productivity: both low labor productivity and low total factor productivity.

Thus, at the same time that China and India were said to benefit from their comparatively low unit-labor costs, Mexico was said to suffer from a situation in which its unit-labor costs approximated those of the United States; the wage was almost a tenth of what it was in the United States, but so was average productivity. If the mode of thought implied in the Heckscher-Ohlin model were correct, Mexico would be, from the standpoint of its representative position in the international division of labor, half the world: the labor rich ready to trade with the capital rich. But it was not half the world. It was just a failure in a particular place: Mexico had failed to find a way either to cheapen its labor or sufficiently to raise its labor productivity, as well as its total factor productivity.

If the most advanced practices and technologies of production can be established anywhere, combined with either cheaper or dearer labor, the road is open to choose and to develop specialized positions within the world division of labor rather than to accept such positions as part of the destiny of established comparative advantage or as a rung in a ready-made ladder of economic ascent from labor-intensive to capital-intensive production. The hope of reaping the benefits of increasing returns to scale will simply widen a margin of maneuver resulting from other causes.

A second fact concerns the return to labor, its share in national income. The return to labor varies starkly among countries at comparable levels of economic development and average productivity. No idea commands broader acceptance in contemporary applied economics than the idea that the real wage cannot over the long term be made to rise more quickly than labor productivity. All attempts to make it rise more quickly will fail; inflation will turn real gains into nominal ones. This belief comes from the same idea world as the gold standard and the pre-Keynesian "sound-finance doctrine" of the early twentieth century, yet it has mysteriously survived their downfall. It is in fundamental agreement with a characteristic tenet of Marxist economic theory, according to which the "rate of surplus value"—the part of value that the labor-buying capitalist can extract from the labor-selling worker and keep for himself—converges in capitalist economies. It is a belief enjoying such widespread acceptance and authority that it should come as no surprise to find that it is false. The limited element of truth it contains helps conceal the falsehood of the rest.

A close proxy for the Marxist concept of surplus value is the familiar statistical measure of the proportion of wages to value added in the industrial sector of a national economy. Countries at similar levels of economic and technological development, and therefore also of average total factor productivity as well as labor productivity, show striking differences in the wage take of value added in the industrial sector—the inverse of what Marx called "surplus value." In a recent study, this percentage was 65 percent for Denmark (2003), 62 percent for Germany (2003), 57 percent for South Africa (2004), 50 percent for the United Kingdom (2003), 32 percent for the United States (2002), 27 percent for Japan (2002), 23 percent for India (2004), and 21 percent for Brazil (2004).* It was generally higher for developed and lower for developing countries. Striking differences emerge, however, between countries at similar levels of development and productivity. Some of these differences can be attributed to different scarcities of land, labor, and capital as well as to the relative importance of natural resource extraction to each national economy. Nevertheless, much

---

*UNIDO (United Nations Industrial Development Organization) Industrial Statistics online database on Employment, Wages, and Related Indicators, January 26, 2007.

of the difference remains even after we have given these conditions their due.

The rest is politics. The legal and institutional position of capital has, we may conjecture, a residual and substantial role in shaping the relations among government, capital, and labor. The wide disparities in the part of national income enjoyed by labor could never have arisen in the first place if the relation between the productivity of labor and the return to labor had a natural history independent of collective action and political initiative, if, despite being a fact about society rather than about nature, this relation were beyond the reach of the will.

The truth in the dogma that the real wage cannot outpace the rise in productivity is the futility of attempts to achieve by fiat rises in the real wage. A legislated rise in the proportion of national income won by labor can work. However, it can work only when sustained by rights and arrangements shifting power toward workers while maintaining competitive pressure in product, capital, and labor markets. The falsehood in the dogma is the denial of the power of change in institutions and policies to produce such an effect.

The relation of these realities to the tradition of thought that arose out of Ricardo's doctrine of comparative advantage and that found classic expression in the Heckscher-Ohlin model may be indirect. It is nevertheless of decisive importance. The direction of specialization within the world economy will be influenced by the rewards of labor as well as by its productivity. Contrary to the half-true dogma, each of these may vary independently of the other, and it may do so not just for a while and for a little bit but lastingly, cumulatively, and dramatically.

The political construction of the relative status and reward of labor relative to capital confirms what we already know from other observations and arguments: that to a much larger extent than the main line of thinking about comparative advantage would allow, the specialized place of a national economy within the world economy can be chosen rather than discovered. It is not a fate; it is a project, forged in the face of constraint and on the anvil of contests of interest and of vision.

A third large fact to be accommodated by a revised view of comparative advantage and productive specialization within the world economy is the open-ended and two-sided relation of increases in the return of labor to the economic rise of nations. An increase in the real wage, pushed by politics and institutions beyond the limits of productivity gains, may form part of a narrative of economic regression. Thus, for example, the Mexico of today is a country that has failed to achieve sustained increases in either labor or total factor productivity but is unable or unwilling to cheapen its labor to Chinese or Indian levels. Its high unit-labor costs—with low productivity and a wage that is low but not low enough—falls as a dead hand on its economic future.

Upward pressure on the returns to labor, even pressure to give labor proportionately more than prior advances in productivity justify, may, however, be part of a story of progressive economic revolution. It may help, and in many historical circumstances it has helped, accelerate inventions and innovations from which gains in productivity result. It may hasten the substitution of the activities we have already learned how to repeat by the machines that can repeat them, and save more of the time and talent of more people for the activities that we do not yet know how to repeat. Then the intrinsic attractions of increases in the returns to labor in rescuing more people from poverty and indignity will be magnified by their place in a greater effort to lift from human life the burdens of drudgery and stupefaction.

What way of organizing a national economy will make it more likely for the benign effect to prevail over the prejudicial consequence? The relative enhancement of the position and of the rewards of labor must be part of a larger impulse, in the economy and in culture, in firms and in schools, to turn production into learning and cooperative work into collective experimentation. The experimentation must include experimentation with the forms of the market economy and of representative democracies as the two large sets of arrangements by which we can advance without blueprints.

What approach to the organization of international commerce will form a setting hospitable to such a turn? It must be one in which the reconciliation of alternative strategies and directions in the making of such experiments, rather than the simple maximization of free trade, becomes the commanding principle of the global trade regime. It must also be one in which the universalization of ever more exacting labor standards generalizes upward pressure on returns to labor to the whole of the world.

CHAPTER 3

Ideas

● ○ ●

In Search of a Point of View

To find an intellectual direction that can illuminate these historical experiences and clarify these conceptual problems, we must think beyond the boundaries of ideas that address free trade alone. We cannot do justice to the debate about free trade and protection from within the categories in which this debate has traditionally been framed.

In this chapter I offer six ideas as starting points for a way of thinking, not just about international trade but also about economic activity in general—building blocks for a different approach. Without a struggle to develop such an approach, my explanatory accounts and programmatic proposals about the world division of labor would be groundless and arbitrary, or they would be condemned to remain parasitic on the terms of a controversy that has long become sterile.

Each of the first three ideas informs one of the main theses I put forward in the next chapter. The fourth idea makes explicit an assumption on which two of the first three rely. The fifth idea is the one that has the most far-reaching theoretical and practical implications for the debate about free trade, yet also has the least obvious connection with it. The sixth idea puts the previous five in the context of a broader view of mind and work.

Specialization and Discovery: When Competition Inhibits Self-Transformation

The first idea addresses the countervailing interests at stake in the debate about free trade. It is an idea about collective learning and about the difference between the circumstances in which uncontrolled competition with more advanced competitors encourages learning and the circumstances in which such competition prevents learning. This first idea amounts to an interpretation of what the classical quarrel over free trade was always about, restated in the language of concerns that contemporaries have come to view as paramount.

To become specialized in particular lines of production, on the basis of natural or achieved comparative advantage, and yet to be goaded into improvement and innovation by continuing contact with more advanced producers—with those who produced more value with less labor—whether in those lines of production or in other lines requiring greater capital and knowledge: such was one of the essential benefits of free trade, according to the classical doctrine. Under competitive pressure, you would learn, as a country, as a sector of the economy, or as firm, to do better what you already did, or to make something new that the world valued more. The daily realities of trade with those who produced different things, as well as of competition with those who produced the same or similar things, would constantly present you with inspirations and incentives to self-improvement.

The efficiency that you achieve through specialization within an international division of labor will help you progress, both by improving how you produce what you already produce and by showing you how to move from one line of activity to another, more gainful and more demanding of capital and skill.

The core of this first idea is that there are certain recurrent situations in which this dream is likely to be realized and others in which it is just as likely to be frustrated. The difference between these two sets of situations turns on the relation in each of them among three conditions: the benefit of becoming specialized, the value of being challenged, the danger of being overwhelmed.

There are two polar situations in which the dream can be most readily realized: when your trading partners are much more advanced than you are and when they are more or less as advanced as you are. If they are much more advanced than you are, you can hope to become more efficient and productive—especially by moving into more labor-saving lines of business or forms of production—without either threatening them or being threatened by them. The constant example of their organizational and technological refinement, made patent in the daily realities of trade, will hold before you a standard that, although it may be unreachable in the short term, will nevertheless mark the direction in which you should move.

Now consider the situation when your trading partners are at a level of development—and especially of command over capital, knowledge, and the replacement of repetitive labor by machines—similar to your own. Once again, as in the circumstance of radical inequality with your trading partners, the benefits of specialized production need not be enjoyed at the cost of the possibilities of self-improvement. You and your trading partners may at any moment enter into one another's lines of business. This ceaseless competition will make its victims: the firms that stand to lose their lead, and all the workers they employ. Nevertheless, in the face of these localized, shifting, and ephemeral defeats, you and your trading partners alike will be able to draw on a common stock of resources: the capital, the machines, the skills, the practices, the organizational arrangements, and the enacted ideas that place you and them at a comparable level of development.

But what if you and your trading partners are at unequal—but not very unequal—levels of development? In particular, what if you are the relatively more backward economy and your partners are the relatively more advanced ones? Your paths are then much more likely to cross theirs than they would be if the difference in development between you and them were stark. The situation will in this respect more closely resemble the circumstance of relative equality: you will have the prospect of moving into lines of business in which they hold strong, even entrenched places.

However, the situation will differ from that circumstance of relative equality in two important ways. For one thing, in the course of your advance you will have to cross a dangerous terrain of transition during which you may have to compete in certain fields of production without enjoying the same productivity of labor as your relatively more advanced competitors. You will consequently be forced to rely on cheap labor. You will do so in the hope that this reliance will not prevent you from continuing to move up the ladder of labor-saving technology and organization.

For another thing, you will be less able to draw on the resources that enable your partners, in their dealings with one another, quickly to replace failure in one domain with success in others. Your stock of resources and capabilities for such substitutions will be more restricted. You may be forced to fall back on the relative cheapness of your labor as your sole compensation. It will be a perilous reliance because it may tempt you to slow or to postpone the adoption of labor-saving technologies and practices. As a result, you may take longer to shift the focus of time and attention in your society away from the activities you know how to repeat, and therefore know how to embody in formulas and machines, toward those activities that you have not yet learned how to repeat. Yet it is precisely this shift, from repetition to novelty and to the power of creating it, that matters most to the ability of a society to respond to the failure of an established line of production by replacing it with something else.

Your relatively more advanced trading partners will also be threatened. Your forced reliance on cheaper and less productive labor will crack a whip usefully at their backs, forcing them to quicken the pace by which formulas and machines come to replace whatever part of labor and production they have learned how to model as a set of repetitious operations. However, the social cost of this acceleration will not be evenly distributed throughout their societies; it will fall most heavily on the part of the labor force doing the work that the catchers-up have now taken up as their own. If the victims fail to react successfully, economic growth will go on under the shadow of increasing inequality and exclusion. If the victims do react, economic growth may be interrupted by social strife.

What this thought experiment suggests is that the different elements of collective learning, in and through competitive specialization under an international division of labor, are not foreordained to work with one another. They may work against one another. The likelihood of their working in one way rather than another will be shaped by the relative powers of whole national economies as well as by the relative capabilities of particular firms. The greatest tension—productive of an antagonism of interests that the dogmas of free trade may be unable to resolve—will arise when inequality among the partners is real but not radical: when the emergent face the established.

Politics over Economics: When Restraints on Trade Imply No Surrender to Special Interests or Costly Dogmas

A second idea concerns the relation between economics and politics. The range of alternative lines of response on which a society can draw when confronted by dilemmas such as those exposed by the first idea is not determined within the economy itself. It is determined by politics. More precisely, it is formed by the combination of two distinct but connected factors, both of them political in nature.

One factor is the extent to which the state is able credibly to represent the wide interests of society at large rather than the narrow interests of a faction or a class with privileged influence on government. The second factor is the degree to which the practices of politics and of policy, giving content to the conception of the collective interests, are experimental in character, organizing a process of sustained social discovery of ends as well as of means, of values as well as of interests, of collective self-understandings as well as of national strategies.

The creation of such a state and of such a practice of politics and policy is unfinished business in the historical experience of humanity. Even the most vibrant democracies in the most egalitarian contemporary societies realize this ideal very imperfectly. At their most egalitarian, those societies continue to be shaped by a coexistence between class and meritocracy, with vast disparities between the power and influence of different groups. At their most vibrant, those democracies continue to rely on a narrow stock of institutional arrangements and ideas, limiting their ability to subject social privilege to popular pressure.

Public administration continues to be organized on a model of command and control: the administrative equivalent to mass-production industry, with its stark hierarchies of conception and execution, its rigid contrasts among specialized jobs, its trust in standardization as the condition of efficiency achieved through scale, its segregation of cooperation and competition into wholly separate domains of experience, and its treatment of innovation as episodic interruption rather than ongoing practice. It is as if warfare had continued to be dominated by the massed and brittle infantry formations of the eighteenth century. As a result, the making and implementation of policy cease to be sources of discovery, and become instruments for the imposition of dogma, top down.

These constraints on democratic deepening and administrative practice radically limit the range of options with which a society can respond to problems and tensions like those that the first idea identifies in the relation between the benefits of specialized production and the requirements of economic self-improvement. They force a country to make a Hobson's choice between relinquishing all restraints on free trade, even when relative advantage may justify such restraints, and imposing the restraints at the risk of allowing them to serve powerful interests and costly dogmas.

The accumulation of such Hobson's choices becomes a kind of fate, unconsciously accepted as the closed horizon within which practical argument about economic policy must move. Even if selective and temporary restraints on trade may seem justifiable in theory, they will be denounced in practice as an invitation to the evils of playing favorites and of riding hobbyhorses instead of letting the market discover the most efficient solutions. The result will be a utopian view of the market economy as a machine capable of discovering Pareto-improving solutions through decentralized experimentation, so long as it remains free of discrete instances of market failure.

The counterpart to this utopian view of the market is a dystopian view of the state—and of all forms of collective action not governed by market forces, a view seeing government and collective organization undisciplined by the market as tools of special interest and factional prejudice. The utopian and the dystopian views work together, lending credence to the belief that the political adjustments of economic forces that may seem best in theory will rarely be best in practice. In no field is this lesson more insistently urged than in debates about international trade.

Consider now the relation of these background assumptions to the traditional debate about free trade and protection. Restraints on free trade, so the argument goes, may be justified in theory— for example, by considerations such as those that underlie the first idea or by any of the traditional justifications of protection developed in the course of the long history of debates about free trade. However, all such restraints amount to exercises of political selection trumping a resource allocation generated by the market—the market as it is presently organized. Selective tariffs are, in one fundamental sense, like selective interest rates or selective exchange rates, or selective subsidies. They ordinarily serve a factional interest: whatever interest, or combination of interests, succeeds in winning power or influencing government. They will give voice to dogma: whatever belief about national development enjoys the prestige of passing fashion. The factional interests and the prestigious dogmas are all too likely to converge—the former speaking in the language of the latter—to the detriment of the collective stake in unrestrained competition and surprising discovery.

The extent to which selective policy, including selective protection, represents an invitation to the twin evils of favoritism and dogmatism is not, however, invariant. It is a variable. It varies according to the institutional arrangements that organize government and policy making. To gain an initial impression of the significance of such variation, we require no broader view of the alternative ways in which democratic politics, market economies, and free civil societies might be organized. All we need is an open-minded appreciation of variations that already exist.

For example, the northeast Asian economies of the latter part of the twentieth century were famously adept at the centralized formulation of trade and industrial policy, for the most part top down, by a national bureaucracy. To a large extent, this approach to trade and industrial policy remained in the grip of dogma, immune to experimental challenge and revision and therefore susceptible to costly mistakes. However, even within this narrow historical sample the infirmity was not uniform: it beset Korea, for instance, more than Taiwan because policy making in the latter engaged a wider circle of small and medium-sized firms than it did in the former.

When we turn from the danger of riding hobbyhorses to its twin, the peril of playing favorites, we find that a shared characteristic of the northeast Asian "tiger economies" of the second half of the twentieth century was their half-conscious attachment to a particular way of weakening the influence of powerful factional interests over public policy. The distinctive character of the approach they embraced stands out very clearly by comparison to the direction taken in most of the Latin American countries of the same historical period. In those societies, the traditional forms of liberal democracy, imported from richer and less unequal societies, were unable effectively to channel the political energy of the people and consequently unable as well to prevent the periodic suppression of republican institutions. No independent bureaucracy with any substantial autonomy from the plutocracy, or from the other powerful interests in societies, could form and gain strength in such an environment. Government was for the most part too "soft", too pliant to these interests, to subordinate them to a strategic vision.

By contrast, the northeast Asian economies saw the implementation of trade and industrial policy on the basis of limited or guided democracy and more generally of a form of education, culture, and consciousness discouraging nonconformity. The state was relatively "hard." Its hardness enabled it to limit its vulnerability to the evil of dogmatism, but at a mounting cost. Authoritarianism in politics and antiexperimentalism in culture limited the ability of society to invent alternatives and to try them out, in the large and in the small, in trade as well as in every other domain of public policy and social life. These attributes, the conditions of temporary success, would in time become causes of failure.

There was then, however, no easy way out: the struggle to democratize the state and to render culture more experimental would create strife and confusion before they could ensure, on a changed basis, new clarity and capability. Whether state, society, and culture could be more thoroughly opened to democratic experimentalism depended on the invention of political institutions and social practices that were not established even in the most successful and vibrant democracies of the day. What was missing was a state made less pliant to privilege by the radicalization rather than by the limitation of democracy. What was missing as well was a form of education connecting capability with resistance and anchoring insight into the actual in the imagination of the possible. The conditions were lacking for administrative arrangements and practices of policy that could contain the twin evils of dogmatism and favoritism.

A high-energy democracy favors a sustained and inclusive heightening of organized political mobilization. It provides for rapid resolution of impasse among the political branches of government. It encourages experimentation, in particular sectors and localities, with countermodels to the main line of law and policy. Such a state need not achieve resistance to capture by powerful interests at the expense of rigidity in creating and confronting social and economic alternatives. Recalcitrance to favor in turn facilitates resistance to dogma. It then becomes easier to develop a practice of policy that is pluralistic rather than unitary, ready to propagate successful local practice rather than to impose a foreordained blueprint, open to challenge and participation from below and outside, and determined to split the difference between deliberation and spontaneity.

This thought experiment suggests the flaw in the idea that what is best in theory—if it involves, as restraints on trade do, selection and direction—is unlikely to prove the best in practice, given the ease with which government may serve as a tool of private grabbing and public blindness. The flaw is that this view disregards or downplays existing as well as possible variation in ways of organizing politics and policy. Whether a form of selective policy that may appear attractive in principle will also prove superior in experience may depend on where it fits in a spectrum of alternative methods and arrangements—or on whether its architects succeed in broadening this spectrum.

The theoretical and practical significance of this point increases vastly when we connect it with a more general idea. The idea is that the forms of representative democracy, of the market economy, and of free civil society now established in the rich North Atlantic countries represent a subset of a larger and open-ended set of institutional possibilities. There is no direct or self-evident passage, by way of either analytic inference or evolutionary constraint, from the abstract conception of a representative democracy, a market economy, or a free civil society to any of the particular sets of contingent institutional arrangements with which such institutional abstractions have been historically associated. The chance that a form of selectivity that appears to be best in theory may also be, or may become, best in practice now appears a corollary of this general proposition.

However, the institutional arrangement of the market is not at the same level, or does not have as much importance, as the institutional organization of democracy. The market cannot create its own presuppositions, including the institutions and practices by which it is organized and the endowments of the individuals who move within it. It is politics—in the large sense of the contest over the terms of social life as well as over the mastery and uses of governmental power—that determines these presuppositions. Politics, by contrast to the market, does create its own presuppositions—it crowns itself—although it does so within the constraints imposed by the stock of available resources and ideas.

From this line of reasoning, it follows that the extent to which what is best in theory can also be best in practice is set outside the economy. The contingent limitations of politics and policy making shape it. The deepening of democracy, through the renovation of its institutional forms, increases the likelihood that what is best in theory—for example, the restraints on trade that may be justified in the circumstance of relative backwardness—may also be best in practice.

A discussion of trade policy—or indeed any other branch of practical economic argument—that leaves politics out will not simply be incomplete. It will inevitably lead to misleading conclusions. However, we cannot fill this gap by importing ideas from political science; the established political science is, for the most part, like the established economic analysis. It is deficient in the quality that we now most require: the denial to the established ways of organizing markets and democracies of their mendacious semblance of naturalness and necessity. Unable to rely on a ready-made alternative intellectual practice, we must develop the practice we need as we go along, from the inside out and from the bottom up.

Order and Revision: When Free Trade Strengthens the Capacity for Self-Transformation

A third idea has to do with the relation between the way a trading regime develops and the ability of the participants in such a regime to change themselves. A remarkable feature of the established way of thinking about free trade is that it treats these two processes as unconnected, except to the extent that more trade is supposed to bring about faster improvement under the prodding of specialization, competition, and emulation.

Suppose, however, the following contrary hypothesis. For any given level of trade or free trade, the trading regime may be so designed that it either strengthens or weakens the capacity of the trading partners to reorganize themselves, experimentally, as they go along. The constraint on self-transformation addressed by this hypothesis is not the constraint resulting from a given degree of openness to trade, as measured either by the level of protection or by the relation between a country's aggregate trade flows and its gross domestic product. It is the constraint resulting from the particular way a trading regime is organized, at whatever level of openness it may provide. What matters, from the standpoint of this hypothesis, is not how much free trade but what kind of free trade.

Consider a simple example, of great theoretical and practical importance. It rests on an assumption about the open-ended diversity of possible forms of a market economy. This assumption forms the core of one of the recurrent ideas in my argument. As a system of free trade develops, its rules may impose on the participants in the trading regime a particular version of the market economy: a definite approach to the content, sources, and scope of contract and property rights, a way to uphold the barrier separating government from private enterprise, and even a certain treatment of the rights of investors and shareholders.

The result will be to associate the advancement of free trade with a narrowing funnel of institutional convergence among the trading partners. It will be to restrict their capacity for self-revision except insofar as self-revision results from greater freedom to trade. The evolution of a trading regime may also follow an opposite tack, putting institutional minimalism in the place of such an institutional maximalism; it may prefer arrangements that leave the greatest possible latitude open to the trading partners in deciding what type of economy—indeed, what type of market economy—to establish.

This room for institutional divergence among the trading partners, built into the rules of the trading regime, will in turn increase the likelihood that the trading system will itself require more complication and permit more revision: ongoing experimentation with the rules of the worldwide trading system as well as with the institutional arrangements of each trading partner. Instead of organizing trade among trading partners that are more and more alike, it will have to organize trade among partners that are persistently or increasingly different, in their practices and institutions as well as in their endowments and specializations.

The core of this third idea is that we should never think about free trade simply in the one dimension of relative freedom to trade and of restraint on trade. We should think of it as well in a second dimension: at whatever level of freedom or restraint, how much freedom for self-revision does the trade regime grant to the trading parties and how much restraint on self-revision does it impose on them.

In principle, the best type of free trade will be the type associating more free trade with more opportunity for self-revision. The worst type will be the type connecting more free trade with less opportunity for self-revision. The first type will promote the market-based logic of decentralized experimentalism in one dimension while undercutting it in another. The second type will express in both dimensions the same experimentalist impulse.

Consider this notion in its most generalized form, as an idea about practices, institutions, and assumptions in general rather than merely about trade or even about the economy as a whole. We can distinguish two classes of activities: the ordinary moves we make within a framework of assumptions and arrangements that we take as given, and the extraordinary moves by which we challenge and revise pieces of such a framework.

The distance between these two classes of activities may be greater or smaller. The framework may be organized to resist criticism and change and to win for itself a semblance of naturalness, necessity, and authority. It may begin to seem part of the furniture of the world; the structures it establishes will then seem as if they were natural facts rather than the frozen fighting and the petrified inventions that all social structures really are. A social or natural calamity may be needed to change such an order and to rob it of its delusive semblance of naturalness. Catastrophe will become the requirement of transformation.

By contrast, the framework may be organized to facilitate its revision and diminish the dependence of change on crisis. The distance between our context-preserving and our context-changing moves will then shrink. Changing the context, step by step and piece by piece, will become part of our normal activity.

Our stake in moving from the first situation to the second, from the naturalization to the denaturalization of the institutional and cultural settings in which we think and move, is deep and pervasive. It touches on our most fundamental interests. It is causally related to our economic interest in being able more freely to recombine people and resources: our practical experimentalism remains limited so long as we are prevented from experimenting with the setting within which, and with the practices by which, we experiment. It has a causal connection to our social interest in the disentanglement of cooperation from social division and hierarchy: no system of social division and hierarchy can remain in place that fails to prevent the arrangements and presuppositions on which it depends from perpetual questioning, tinkering, and attack. It directly expresses our spiritual interest in being able to participate, wholeheartedly and even single-mindedly, in a social world without surrendering to it our powers of criticism, resistance, and transcendence.

When we understand and practice the freedom to recombine factors of production only within an institutional organization of production and exchange that we accept as the natural or necessary form of a market economy, we impose on the exercise of this freedom an arbitrary and burdensome restraint. It remains caged within a structure that fails to bear the imprint of its spirit or to do justice to its potential. Once deepened or radicalized, freedom to recombine factors of production for the sake of greater efficiency or total factor productivity would come to include a freedom to rearrange and renovate the arrangements forming the institutional setting of production and exchange. Different regimes of private and social property might, for example, coexist experimentally within the same market economy.

Translated into the conception of a regime of international trade, this approach to thinking about an economy results in the proposition with which I began the statement of this third idea. The best such regime will be the one that, at any level of the freedom to trade for which it provides, also imposes the least restraint on the ability of its participants—trading economies as well as individual firms—to reorganize themselves.

Alternative Free Trade, Alternative Globalizations: The Market Liberated from the Doctrine of the Market

A fourth idea concerns the relation between the concept of a market economy and the institutional arrangements by which it is organized. More generally, it addresses the relation between abstract institutional concepts, such as the market or democracy, and their tangible institutional expressions. This fourth idea is a presupposition of both the second and the third ideas; I have anticipated it in the course of presenting them. Until we appreciate its force, we cannot hope to rid ourselves of the superstitions that confuse debates about free trade.

The gist of this idea is that the market has no single natural and necessary form. No ideal limit exists to which market economies around the world must, should, or could converge. If convergence occurs in one historical period, it will be reversed in another; it will lack a basis in deep-seated and universal forces.

The principle bears generalization: it applies, in a similar way, to all other abstract institutional ideas: for example, the idea of a representative democracy. The meaning we habitually ascribe to any such institutional conception or ideal will be the product of a double reference, to a set of interests, values, or aspirations—an understanding of our collective stake in the institutional project that the notion evokes—and to a set of concrete, contingent arrangements with which we ordinarily associate the conception or ideal.

So long as practical and ideological conflict fails to escalate, the two references will appear to form a seamless whole: the stake we have in the idea will seem naturally expressed in the particular arrangements with which we associate it. This impression of seamlessness, however, is only an illusion, made possible by relative stagnation. Under the pressure of escalating practical or ideological strife and invention, we come to recognize that the familiar institutional vehicle could be stretched in different directions and changed in different ways. The changes in the institutional vehicle in turn make us aware of tensions and ambiguities in the interests and in the ideals that seemed naturally and necessarily realized in the established arrangements. What appeared to be a unity begins to unravel, in the mind and in reality.

Not only is there no single natural and necessary way in which a market economy can be organized, there is also no closed list of possible types of a market economy, or of a representative democracy, or of a free civil society, or indeed of any general institutional

project. All such projects remain subject to the potential dishar-
monies and transformations of the double reference. What we face
is a penumbra of possibility around present and past experience:
getting to somewhere else from where we are now, by taking steps
within our reach.

The idea that the market economy has no single determinate
expression in law or institutions is an old insight. In fact, it may
have been the single most insistent revelation to have resulted
from the evolution of legal thought in the West from the middle
of the nineteenth century to the middle of the twentieth. Early
nineteenth-century jurists had set out to demonstrate that a
single coherent and gapless system of rules of private law, and
of supporting public-law institutions, could be derived by quasi-
deductive inference from the abstract idea of a market or of a free
society.

However, in trying to confirm this proposition, the jurists established its opposite: their self-subversion was the badge of their
seriousness. Contrary to their aims, they ended up showing that
at each step toward greater institutional detail, the institutional
abstractions whose supposedly predetermined content they had
set out to reveal could take different turns. Each of these turns
would have different consequences not only for the distribution
of wealth, income, and opportunity but also for the organization
of economic growth and popular government. Which turns were
to be preferred was not something that could be established by
analyzing the idea of a market or the concepts of property and
contract; the choice depended on conjectures, informed by inconclusive experience. It had consequences for the struggle for
wealth, income, and power. It required taking a position in a contest of visions of the possible and desirable forms of social order
and experience.

Insight into the institutional indeterminacy of the market economy formed a vital part of the conceptual background to a momentous turn in the legal thought and practice of the twentieth
century. You could not have a free society by simply clinging to a
foreordained system of private rights. It was necessary to ask who
in fact had the opportunity and the means to exercise the rights.

The rights depended for their reality on conditions that might fail—indeed, regularly did fail—to be satisfied: the requirements for their practical enjoyment might be missing, or denied to large classes of people. Thus all law, including the law organizing the market economy, would have to be dialectically arranged into two parts. One part would consist of rules and arrangements organizing individual initiative. The other part would ensure that inequalities of power, of wealth, information, access and opportunity never became so extreme and entrenched as to turn the first half of the law, the half shaping the exercise of individual self-determination, into a sham.

This dialectical reorganization of the law came up against a limit, of efficacy as well as of insight, that it has yet to overcome. A society can take different directions in identifying and overcoming obstacles to the reality of the rights of economic freedom. By taking one direction rather than another it becomes one kind of society, one kind of economy, one kind of market order rather than another.

The simple idea that the market economy can assume different legal and institutional forms, that it has no single natural and necessary expression, has never fully penetrated, to this day, the practice of economic analysis and the course of policy debate. It is to be distinguished from the recognition of specific market failures resulting from inequalities of power and asymmetries of information. Moreover, it leads directly to the conclusion that in dealing with a market economy we are not restricted to regulating it or to compensating for its inequalities, after the fact, through redistributive tax-and-transfer. We can reshape it, changing some of the rules and arrangements that make it what it is.

Thus developed, awareness of the diversity of institutional forms of a market economy has two applications to the debate about free trade in a global economy.

The first application has as its subject the idea of the international trading system as a regime of free trade among economies that are themselves free: that is to say, market economies. It is an application to which we come by combining two ideas. One is the idea of the diversity of institutional forms of a market economy.

Another is that free trade regimes may differ in the freedom of self-revision that they allow to their participants. At any given level of openness to trade, the more freedom of self-revision, the better.

No experiment with a particular line of production within a market economy is likely to be as important as experiments about the organization of a market economy. Instead of meaning ever fewer restraints on commerce among institutionally convergent market economies, free trade can come to mean less restrained commerce among institutionally divergent market economies. I have described the grounds for preferring this latter project to the former.

The second application of the idea of the institutional indeterminacy and diversity of the market has as its subject the world trading system itself. If a market economy can be organized in different ways, so can a universal order of free trade among market economies. Under such a revised view of increasing economic openness in the world, countries do not undertake to obey an institutional formula, of either international trade or national economic organization, simply because they have committed themselves to become and to remain market economies.

The effort to develop an open world economy has the same characteristic with which the jurists of the nineteenth century had to contend in their own effort to translate the abstraction of a free economic order into legal and institutional detail: you cannot justify the choice of one route over another by claiming that it is the market route. There are too many market routes. You need a view of the relation of trade to growth, and of growth to other interests and values. You need such a view as much to work out the conception of universal free trade as to define the organization of a market economy in any one country.

We are not limited to having simply more market or more regulation and command, according to the simple hydraulic model that has been the obsessive theme of ideological debate for the past two hundred years. We can reimagine and remake the market economy. Similarly, globalization, which has free trade as its practical and conceptual core, is not there on a take-it-or-leave-it basis. We are not confined to having more of it or less, to making it go faster or slower. We can have it on different terms, but only by changing how we understand and organize free trade.

The Division of Labor Reimagined and Remade: From the Pin Factory to the Factory of Innovation

A fifth idea addresses the division of labor. It considers the division of labor at any scale and scope, all the way from the division of labor at a work station, in a factory, a shop, or an office, to the division of labor in a global economy. Worldwide free trade among countries, on the basis of specialized production and natural or achieved comparative advantage, is, after all, a species of the division of labor. Our assumptions about the division of labor inevitably inform our ideas about international trade. We need to correct some of those assumptions.

The pin-factory model of the division of labor that we trace back to Adam Smith and that found its most fulsome expression in Henry Ford's assembly line no longer does justice to the realities and the possibilities of what is sometimes called the "technical" division of labor: the way work gets organized at the work station. We can best understand that model as the limiting case of a much broader range of ways of organizing work. Having wrested ourselves free of the stranglehold of that limiting picture, we can come to see the division of labor in a different light, and revise our view of what makes some of its forms more promising and productive than others. This insight in turn changes how we think about international trade.

In Adam Smith's fabled pin factory, the division of labor took the form of a rigid specialization of tasks, under stark hierarchical supervision. The counterpart to rigid contrasts among specialized tasks in the making of pins was the equally stark opposition between those who commanded or monitored, from on top, and those who obeyed, at the bottom, endlessly repeating their appointed rounds.

Such a way of organizing work seemed justified by irresistible advantages. A worker could become proficient at one maneuver rather than being indifferently skilled at many. That most valuable of resources, time, could be saved by avoiding the need to move from one task to another. The point was to use repetition to save time.

The pin-factory model of the division of labor gained much of its appeal from its implicit connection with a particular view of the constraints on economic growth. According to this view, widely shared up to the twentieth century, the most important of such constraints was the size of the surplus society extracted and reserved over current consumption. The surplus might well have to be extracted coercively; according to Karl Marx, the continuing need for coercive surplus extraction was one of the major justifications not only of the capitalist mode of production but of all class society. The pin-factory approach to the organization of work has been seen as a tool of discipline and repression. It was supposedly needed to impose the sacrifice of present individual pleasures for the sake of future collective wealth.

This view, however, was already anachronistic and misleading when it was first proposed. We know now that the pioneering countries of the "industrial revolution" in late eighteenth- and early nineteenth-century Europe were not distinguished from China at that same period by a higher level of saving; Europe's saving level was lower than China's. They differed by dint of a practice of intellectual, technological, and organizational innovation, made possible by features of society and culture in which the great agrarian-bureaucratic empires ruling much of the rest of the world were deficient.

Consider an alternative view of the division of labor and of the path of its evolution. This view begins not in a distinctive understanding of production but in an idea about the mind. We know how to repeat some of our activities, and we do not know how to repeat others. As soon as we learn how to repeat an activity we can express our insight in a formula and embody the formula in a machine. Our machines can do for us whatever we know how to repeat. They can free our time, energy, and attention for what we have not yet learned how to repeat. In this way we make time count by devoting it, as much as we can, to what does not yet lend itself to formula and repetition.

The not yet repeatable part of our activities—the part for which we lack formulas and therefore also machines—is the realm of innovation, the front line of production. In this realm, production and discovery become much the same thing. We there seek to organize our productive activities so that they become a visible, collective image and instrument of our experimental thinking: our relations to one another in this forward edge of production resemble the problem-solving work of an individual human intellect.

To understand a state of affairs, we must imagine it changed: we must form a view of what it could turn into under certain conditions and by certain interventions. The possible is the adjacent: it is what can come next, as the result of some accessible transformation of a reality that is at hand. We can turn some of these possibilities into things, we can embody experimental conjecture in material production. Production then becomes more than a consequence of experimental thinking, it becomes its embodiment.

The pin-factory model of production describes the organization of work as if labor were a machine, meant to do the things for which we use machines, whatever we have learned how to repeat formulaically. We may have reason to organize work in such a way, but only if labor is abundant and cheap enough, capital is dear enough, machines are scarce and primitive enough, and our time is of little enough value—of so little value that we think we can afford to repeat ourselves. That may indeed be the past of the division of labor. It cannot be its future.

As we begin to free ourselves from the multiple, combined constraints that make the pin-factory model of the organization of labor feasible, we move into another way of understanding and organizing the division of labor: the view of production as collective learning and permanent innovation. Its generative principle is a revolution in our beliefs about the relation of time to the division of labor. The point is no longer to save time by repeating ourselves; it is to save time by avoiding repetition. Standardization—of products and services as well as of productive processes and organizational practices—is the most visible face of repetition.

Under this new dispensation, the tendency of the division of labor will be to weaken rather than to strengthen the hierarchical discontinuities between jobs of supervision and of implementation. The plan of production will be revised in the course of its execution, with the help of all involved, in the light of obstacles and opportunities encountered along the way. Rigid specializations among the roles of the executants will become more fluid, as will sharp contrasts between conception and execution. If the plan of production is revised experimentally on an ongoing basis, so must be the lines dividing different responsibilities in that process. As a result, mastery of a set of core generic and conceptual capabilities, empowering the maximum of resilience, will become more useful than any collection of job-specific, machine-imitating skills.

Such an approach to the division of labor is likely to be realized in broad areas of economic life only if two sets of requirements are met. The first set of requirements is that labor not be so cheap and time so devalued that the pin-factory model of the division of labor remains plausible and attractive. The second set of requirements is that the state and the society support a climate in which innovation-friendly practices of cooperation can flourish.

The form of the division of labor here described as the successor and the antidote to the pin factory is a species of cooperation friendly to innovation; its success depends on a weakening of the tension that normally exists between the disposition to cooperate and the impulse to innovate. When I later return to the theme of innovation-friendly cooperation, I discuss the requirements for its advancement as a mainstay of economic growth and as a point at which our economic interests intersect our higher ends.

This contrast between the two understandings of the division of labor provides an incomplete but powerful standard by which to judge a regime of global trade. Does that particular regime help countries—all countries—to begin, or to continue, the move beyond the pin factory? Or does it, on the contrary, help turn some countries into giant pin factories (or inflexible mass-production machines) while allowing others to specialize in production beyond the pin-factory model?

A regime of international trade may discourage the move beyond the pin-factory model by, for example, the way in which, under the label of "intellectual property," it turns innovations, including innovative processes and methods, into pieces of property. It may do so by inhibiting the worldwide movement of people across national frontiers to such an extent that it helps perpetuate vast disparities in the relative scarcities and price of labor and of capital, pushing some countries to specialize in pin factories while requiring others to do away with all their pin factories. And it may do so simply, and most deeply, by incorporating a particular version of the market economy into the rules establishing universal free trade. Such an incorporation chills the institutional experiments and the untried combinations of private enterprise and governmental initiative that the move from one type of the division of labor to another may require.

This standard of judgment would lose much of its pertinence if it lacked a foothold in a change that the world economy has already undergone. According to a familiar account of the global division of labor, more advanced capital-intensive, and technologically refined production takes place in the core, rich economies. More rudimentary, labor-intensive, and technologically primitive production goes on in the peripheral, developing economies. The hierarchical distribution of production on a worldwide basis is, in this view, the heart and soul of the international division of labor.

Now, however, we find more advanced production established not only in the rich North Atlantic economies but also in the top tier of the developing economies, as much in China, India, and Russia as in the United States, Germany, and Japan. What has flourished in particular sectors is not simply or primarily high-technology, knowledge-intensive industrial production; it is the advanced way of understanding and organizing the division of labor that I earlier contrasted to Smith's pin factory and Ford's assembly line.

These advanced sectors, established all over the world, are in communion with one another. They exchange ideas, practices, and people as well as technologies and services. Their network has, in some measure, already become the commanding force in the world economy. They are responsible for the creation of a growing part of national wealth in many countries, rich or poor.

Nevertheless, these productive vanguards remain only weakly linked to the other parts of their national economies. The vast majority of the labor force in the richer as well as in the poorer countries has no chance of participating in them. The small vanguards and the large rearguards, organized on the basis of contrasting understandings of the division of labor, have increasingly become different and unconnected worlds. The abyss between them has become the source of inequalities that are many-sided in expression and powerful in effect. Such inequalities cannot be adequately redressed by the two devices available in the world for the moderation of economic inequalities: compensatory redistribution by government through tax-and-transfer and the politically supported diffusion of small-scale property.

It is, therefore, not enough to ask of a world trading regime whether it helps each national economy to move beyond the pin factory and to enlarge the range of social and economic life open to innovation-friendly cooperation. It is also important to ask whether a system of trade helps engage the masses of ordinary men and women in the movement from the pin factory to the factory of innovation so that they can stop wasting their time by repeating themselves as if they were machines.

A Central Conception: Mind against Context

Take these ideas for what they are: pieces of an understanding of economic activity in general as well as of international trade in particular. A view of the mind, and thus of our humanity, informs this understanding.*

This conception of the mind and of humanity is not at the same level as the other ideas discussed in this chapter. It penetrates and

---

*For a development of this conception and of the broader philosophical view to which it belongs, see my book, *The Self Awakened: Pragmatism Unbound*, Harvard University Press, 2007.

envelops all of them. It is not so much their foundation as it is their common element. It becomes a little better stated and better grounded each time that one of them advances in refinement and justification. In the context of this conception, each of the ideas explored earlier in this chapter gains deeper meaning.

The mind has two aspects. In one aspect, it is modular and formulaic. The mind is modular in the sense that it consists in separate parts, defined by their distinct functions and embodied in different regions of the brain. The expression of the parts of the mind in parts of the brain is subject to the qualification of plasticity: within certain wide limits, one part of the brain can take on the habitual functions of another. The mind is formulaic (in this its modular aspect) in the sense that these parts act repetitiously according to formulas. It is in this aspect, and only in this aspect, that a mind embodied in a brain is like a set of formulas embodied in a machine.

In this modular and formulaic aspect, the mind is a zombie. It acts under the compulsion of orders. It exhausts its life in repeated moves. If, however, the mind were only a zombie, the characteristic experiences of consciousnessness would remain both inexplicable and impossible. Consciousness is totalizing: it envisages a field of vision, action, and problem solving as a whole and interprets particular incidents in relation to that whole. Consciousness is surprising: it defies containment by any closed system of presuppositions, methods, and canons that can be antecedently stated. Consciousness is transformative: it grasps any particular state of affairs by exploring its transformative variations—what it can turn into under the pressure of certain interventions.

A conscious mind therefore has a second aspect in which it exhibits these totalizing, surprising, and transformative qualities. Here the mind has ceased to be zombie-like. It has become spirit, if by spirit we mean the experience of not being contained or containable by any particular context of life or of thought or by any enumerable list of such contexts. In this second aspect, the mind enjoys the characteristic powers of recursive infinity, nonformulaic initiative, and negative capability. By its power of recursive infinity, it uses finite elements (of language, of thought) to make infinite combinations. By its power of nonformulaic initiative, it makes moves that it does not yet know how to repeat or to bring under a formula. By its power of negative capability, it gains in strength, and adds to insight, by doing more than the habitual, organized settings of its action and thought will countenance. It establishes new contexts for its thought and action.

The consummate expression of this power is the establishment of settings for thought and action that invite this limit-breaking activity and turn it into a device for the ongoing revision of the setting. The result is to attenuate the contrast between being inside a context and being outside it, and to make change less dependent on crisis and the past less able to rule the future.

The relative importance of the two aspects of the mind is not a natural fact that can be measured apart from the historical moment and the social situation. Suppose that society and culture are organized to present themselves as natural facts, entrenched against challenge and change. The distance between the ordinary moves we make within the settled contexts and the extraordinary, crisis-dependent moves by which we change them will widen. The second side of the mind—with its totalizing, surprising, and transformative qualities—will have fewer occasions to express itself. It will remain in the shadows or on the margin. It will depend on exceptional talent and extraordinary occasion.

Now suppose that society and culture are arranged to denaturalize themselves by making themselves more open to criticism and revision. The gap between the routine moves we make within the established settings and the exceptional moves by which we remake them will narrow. The second side of the mind will have more opportunity to manifest itself. It will never occupy the whole of mental life. Nevertheless, it will hold an important position. The relation between the two aspects of the mind will become a matter of paramount importance. It will even emerge as a theme in high culture.

Thus, the relation between the two aspects of the mind is never conclusively determined by nature; it is ultimately determined by politics: by the arrangements of society and culture and, most especially, by the extent to which these arrangements either inhibit or encourage their own revision.

The two-sidedness of the mind expresses and helps constitute a fundamental and pervasive attribute of our humanity, our transcendence over context. To say that we are embodied and situated spirit is to recognize that we are never exhausted by the limited orderings of society and culture, of organization and belief, that we establish and inhabit. They, relative to us, are finite. We, relative to them, are infinite. There is always more in us than there can ever be in them.

We can do more than rebel against the context and reach for the insight, the invention, or the experience that it fails to accommodate. We can create contexts that allow more fully for their own revision than the contexts now established: for example, ways of organizing a market economy or a trading regime that enable us to experiment, sequentially or simultaneously, with alternative regimes of contract and property. As a result, we can loosen the dependence of change on ruin and split the difference between being inside the context and being outside it. We can engage in a particular world without surrendering to it our powers of resistance and reconstruction.

This view of the two aspects of the mind, and the larger conception of humanity with which it is connected, suggest a general approach to the understanding of economic activities and of the division of labor. A few connected and overlapping themes, central to the argument of this book, define this approach.

A first theme is the notion of a contrast between the activities or the forms of labor that we have learned how to repeat and those that we have not. We can describe the repeatable activities in formulas and then embody the formulas in machines. We can use the repetitions, the formulas, and the machines to devote increasing parts of our time and energy to the activities we do not yet know how to repeat. The dialectic between the repeatable and the not yet repeatable is central to our material progress, including the rise of productivity: labor productivity in the first instance, and total factor productivity through the chain of causal connections to which the rise of labor productivity belongs. And it is anchored in the relation between the two sides of the mind.

A second theme is the contrast between two directions in which to arrange the division of labor at work. One direction reduces most of work to the zombie-like activities of the first aspect of the mind, and reserves the totalizing, surprising, and transforming attributes of the second side of the mind to the supervisor or power-holder on top. In this direction lies Adam Smith's pin factory and Henry Ford's assembly line: stark contrasts between supervisory and implementing jobs as well as among the tasks of implementation.

The other direction, the factory of innovation, gives much greater place to the second aspect of the mind in the organization of the mind. It treats the implementation of tasks as an opportunity for their revision, and softens the contrasts between conception and execution as well as among jobs of implementation. It uses our ability to repeat, expressed in formulas that are embodied in machines, to shift more of our time and effort toward the frontier of those activities that we do not yet know how to repeat. In this way, it turns the workplace more nearly into a practical expression of the imagination. (Imagination is only another name for the second aspect of the mind.) In so doing, it also provides in microcosm a model for the remaking of all society.

A third theme is the decisive importance to economic growth of a family of cooperative practices that I have called innovation-friendly cooperation. All forms of material progress, including economic growth, depend on cooperation. A market economy itself, I later argue, is a form of simplified cooperation among strangers that depends on a modicum of trust; such an economy is impossible when there is no trust among the strangers and unnecessary when there is high trust.

However, innovation is almost as important as cooperation. Innovation depends on cooperation: it is impossible to innovate, organizationally or technologically, without securing cooperation. The imperatives of innovation and cooperation nevertheless regularly conflict because every innovation threatens to disturb the vested rights and settled expectations in which any cooperative regime is entangled. A new technology, for example, is likely to be perceived as strengthening the hand of an established or emergent segment of the labor force while threatening the jobs of another segment.

A benefit of great value results when we succeed in designing regimes of cooperation that moderate the tension between cooperation and innovation. The form of the technical division of labor that I called the factory of innovation is itself an expression of such an advance. So, more generally, is any form of cooperation, such as commando warfare, in which the definition of what to do is revised in the course of doing it: all responsible for executing have some share in redefining, and the participants refuse to allow preexisting hierarchies of advantage or allocations of role to restrict how they can work together.

The family of innovation-friendly practices of cooperation depends on conditions that also help shape its character and meaning. Basic educational and economic endowments, with their enabling effect on the individual, must be as universal as possible; they must not depend on holding any particular job. The society, although unbound by any rigid commitment to equality of circumstance, must be relentless in pursuit of equality of opportunity. It must prefer practices and arrangements that destabilize entrenched divisions of role and hierarchies of advantage, whether or not the advantages at issue result from the hereditary transmission of property or of access to high-quality education. The culture must be penetrated by an experimentalist impulse. This impulse must find sustenance in a practice of teaching and learning that is problematic and analytic rather than informational in its method, selective rather than encyclopedic in its scope, cooperative rather than individualist or authoritarian in its social form, and dialectical rather than canonical in its orientation.

Such conditions depend for their fulfillment on the public and private cultivation of the powers associated with the second side of the mind. They in turn help establish a setting in which this aspect of our mental life can become central to our individual and social experience rather than remaining in the shadows.

A fourth theme is the need for a way of thinking about markets and market economies that judges any particular form of market organization by the opportunity it offers for its own ongoing, piecemeal reconstruction, as well as for the free combination of factors of production and the free exchange of what is produced. When we witness increasing freedom to exchange and trade and increasing freedom to combine factors of production, we may be tempted to say that the principal idea of a market economy has been realized. These twin freedoms, however, may be realized in an institutional context—a way of organizing market-oriented exchange and production—that remains largely immunized against challenge and change.

Once we become aware of this hidden constraint, we find ourselves forced to direct our thoughts to a second, unfamiliar level of concern. We need to consider the range of freedom to renovate the institutional framework of market activity as well as to transact within that framework. Our assessment of whether the market principle has been radicalized will now depend on two sets of considerations rather than on one. If advance in freedom at one level—freedom to transact and to combine factors of production—is bought at the cost of failure to advance at the second level—freedom to vary and to revise the transactional setting—we must judge ourselves unsuccessful.

We do not arrive at this way of thinking about markets until we defy a prior premise of much conventional economic thinking: the notion, rarely acknowledged in theory but habitually honored in the practice of analysis and argument, that the market has a single natural and necessary institutional expression. Defiance of this notion may seem sterile. It provides support, however, to the way of thinking about markets I have just described. It becomes fertile through its marriage with the imagination of alternative institutional forms of a market economy.

The two-level thinking about markets that results is incompatible with much in our received assumptions about free trade. It will not be enough for an international trading regime to lower barriers to trade if, in so doing, it hinders experiment and diversity in the way each of the trading partners arranges production and exchange and organizes its own market economy.

The more we approach trade in particular and market-oriented activity in general with an eye to these two levels of concern rather than just to one, the greater the likelihood that our proposals will make the world safer for the second side of the mind. The best framework—including the best framework for global trade—will be the one that is least a prison, even if this prison has graven over its entrance the word freedom. It will therefore also be the one that offers the most propitious home for our powers of recursive infinity, nonformulaic initiative, and negative capability.

A fifth theme is that, in the development of economies, the creation of difference is as important as the selection, from the diverse stuff, of the most efficient solutions. As in biological evolution, the results of natural selection depend on the range of variation in the material subject to selection, so in economic history competitive selection depends for its effect on the range and variety of the material to which it applies.

What differences? To specify all the relevant forms of difference, we can begin backward from the output of economic activity, through the processes, practices, machines, and organizations that produce it, until we reach the institutional setting of production and exchange: diversification of goods and services; of ways to join people, ideas, and machines in production and trade; and, finally, of the basic institutional arrangements for market activity, including the regimes of property and contract.

A way of thinking about economic activity that treats the diversification of the material subject to competitive selection as equal in importance to the competitive selection of the most efficient outcomes will differ in orientation and result from one that focuses solely on the latter and takes the former for granted.

The translation of the idea into the practical agenda of development economics helps reveal its intuitive core. Governmental initiative and collective action may be needed to counteract the inhibitions of relative backwardness: for example, the difficulty of using the skills development in one line of production to carry forward another. Not only may the net of productive activities be too thin, the activities by their very backwardness may refuse readily to yield a set of generic, context-transcending capabilities that can be extended to other, neighboring lines of production. For this and other reasons, it may be vital to make up for the missing conditions and deliberately to arouse a fever of creative entrepreneurial activity.

It then becomes all the more important to impose a rigorous selection, through domestic and foreign competition (subject to the qualifications I later explore), of the products of this activity. However, the arousal is as important as the selection; the two must advance together, through a series of successive efforts at overcoming particular constraints on both the supply and the demand sides of the economy. It is just such a coexistence between arousal and selection that this conception generalizes to the economy as a whole. This generalization enables us to treat diversity and efficiency as concerns of equivalent weight in economic thinking.

Like the fourth theme, to which it bears a close relation, the fifth one is connected to the image of the two-sided mind through a view about our relation to the institutional and conceptual contexts of our activity: the same view I invoked when first presenting that image. The deep source of the importance of difference lies in our transcendence over all the particular contexts of our activity. There is always more in us, individually and collectively, than there can ever be in them. From this fact arises our inability ever to find an absolute frame of reference in thought or in social life, one that can accommodate the full scope of our powers and the full range of the experiences that we may have reason to value.

The next best thing to an absolute frame of reference is a frame that facilitates its own remaking and that allows us to engage, on the terms it specifies, without surrendering our powers of criticism, resistance, and revision. To engage without surrendering, and thus to be in the world without being entirely of it, is a fundamental species of freedom and power. The fourth theme, with its emphasis on freedom to change the transactional framework as well as freedom to transact, is directly related to this view.

The fifth theme—the theme of the central importance of the creation of difference in economic life—is connected with a further implication of the same view. Because there is no definitive context for our humanity, including no context that can do justice to our powers of invention and production, we can become bigger only by becoming different: by developing in different directions, by creating different forms of life, by making different things in different ways. A being that faced no such imperative would have no need and no basis for imagination, the second side of the mind. It would have a luxury that we lack: the opportunity to treat diversity—of result, process, and setting—as an assumption rather than as a task. A practice of economic analysis that fails to recognize diversity and efficiency as concerns of equivalent weight misunderstands what economies are and what they can become.

CHAPTER 4

Theses

● ○ ●

Nature of These Theses

The criticisms and ideas explored in the preceding pages animate three theoretical conjectures. These three propositions supply a point of departure for another way of thinking about free trade. I present them informally as empirical speculations, neither conclusively validated by fact nor bereft of support in historical experience. Like any other proposal of an approach to understanding complex phenomena, they should be judged by their theoretical fecundity as well as by their success in illuminating the subject immediately at hand. All three theses have implications for the practice of economic analysis well beyond the scope of the theory of international trade.

The Thesis of Relative Advantage

Restraints on trade are most likely to be justified between trading partners that are neither at roughly equal nor at very unequal levels of development and productivity (total factor productivity as well as labor productivity). Free trade is likely to be most beneficial when practiced between countries that are either at very different levels or at comparable levels of development and productivity. Its harms and dangers are likely to be greatest when it takes place between countries that are at unequal but not extremely unequal levels of development and productivity, such that the relatively more backward economy lies within striking range of the relatively more advanced one. In such a circumstance, the burden will fall chiefly on the relatively more backward economy. I call such a circumstance of countries at different levels of development and productivity, but not at levels so different that the more backward country is unable to move repeatedly into lines of business in which the more advanced one specializes, a situation of relative advantage.

To elaborate this proposition and to grasp the considerations supporting it, I begin by deploying the previously stated ideas about the countervailing relations between efficiency secured through specialization and division of labor on the basis of established comparative advantage and development achieved through emulation, learning, and benchmarking, with the consequent reshaping of comparative advantage.

Consider the pedagogical truism that learning requires pushing the limits of a learner but never overwhelming him by setting before him tasks that lie far beyond his capabilities. Translated into the daily realities of production and productive innovation, this truism points to the importance of what contemporary parlance calls benchmarking. A practice, technology, or arrangement established somewhere else in the world demonstrates, in the course of national and international competition, its superiority to rivals. The question will immediately arise of the extent to which its success depends on local economic conditions that cannot easily be reproduced elsewhere—for example, the cost of labor relative to the cost of other factors of production, in different regions of the world, or the relative proximity of the production process to the inputs it requires. Some of the pertinent favoring circumstances may transcend economics: established traditions of cooperation, craft labor, and education in school, in the family, and at work.

The issue will then always be the same: how to catch up with this "best practice" and reshape it in the process of appropriating it. It is a goal that can be reached only by obeying Piaget's maxim that "to imitate is to invent." The new will have to be combined with the old, the foreign with the local. The localized innovations may turn out to be not so localized after all; the attempt to implement them will put pressure on other practices, interests, and attitudes to which they might at first have seemed irrelevant.

There will be many costs, conflicts, and uncertainties of transition. Whitehead's warning that "it is the business of the future to be dangerous" will apply even to the loveless chores of practical life. It will often be impossible for the imitators and innovators instantly to put the new practices, technologies, or arrangements to a use as efficient as the use for the sake of which they innovated. Things may become worse—that is to say, less efficient and more strife-ridden—before they become better.

The innovators may be able to mitigate the costs of transition by leaning on a crutch, some compensatory advantage to be found in their situation. Of such crutches, the most important—and the most perilous—is lower cost of labor. It is dangerous because the need to shift emphasis from saving of resources to saving of labor has never ceased to play a central part in the movement of innovation and growth.

Such considerations are unlikely to trump the case for free trade among countries that are either at radically different levels of economic development or at comparable levels of economic development. In both these circumstances the advantages of emulation, innovation, and benchmarking under a shield are unlikely to override the benefits of specialized production predicated on established comparative advantage. It is not that in these two contrasting circumstances emulation, innovation, and benchmarking are any less important. It is just that they are less likely to prove incompatible with the countervailing advantages of free, or freer, trade.

In the conditions of countries at radically different levels of economic development, the goods and services that can be produced through the adjacent available steps of innovation are unlikely to come into direct competition with those of the much more advanced trading partner. If they do not differ in character and composition, they will differ radically in the relative cost of the labor required to produce them.

In the circumstances of countries at comparable levels of economic development, innovations, stimulated by emulation and by benchmarking, will normally be compatible with fierce international competition, just as they are compatible with strong domestic competition: trading partners at comparable levels of economic development will not be disabled from the requisite competitive initiatives by challenges lying beyond their grasp. Competition will encourage innovative practices.

This principle will, however, be subject to a qualification of great practical importance. Competitive advantage among economies at comparable levels of development and productivity may result from concentrations of scale and of skill. It may indeed be difficult, costly, and dangerous to enter into a line of business without such preexisting advantages, even when the innovator is at a level of development comparable to that of its trading partner. Here, however, the advocates of free trade have their strong suit. To support restraints on trade for the sake of facilitating the acquisition of new concentrations of scale and skill without the justification of generalized backwardness is to superimpose the dogmas of policy makers on the experiments of entrepreneurs.

In both situations—that of countries at radically different levels of development and that of countries at comparable levels of development—no intractable conflict will exist between competitive advantage secured though international specialization and free trade, on the one hand, and innovation practiced under the spur of imitative benchmarking on the other hand. The trading partners will be able to continue reshaping established comparative advantage through a mix of public action and private enterprise; they will not have to take the existing distribution of comparative advantage for granted. Free trade will be vindicated but on the foundation of a doctrine that treats comparative advantage as a construction: as the product, at once economic and political, of collective and individual genius and invention, not as the dictate of necessity and nature.

By contrast, in the situation of relative advantage, the conflict between the gains of specialization under a regime of free trade and the benefits of innovation under a trade shield are likely to prove most significant and lasting. For it is in this circumstance that the innovators are most likely to face their more advanced competitors without being able or well advised to rely on much lower labor costs or other compensating advantages. Selective protection may then represent a salutary buffer raised over the reformers while they accomplish their work of inventing by imitating. It may keep the challenge below the threshold beyond which it ceases to incite and begins to overwhelm.

No simple metric exists by which to measure striking distance. The choice of phrase is meant to suggest the pragmatic, action-oriented residue in the conception. The relatively backward country is within striking distance of its relatively more advanced trading partners when there is some set of discrete steps by which its production system can reach the level enjoyed by those more advanced partners. The distance is striking distance only if the will to achieve the level is accompanied by a workable understanding of how the goal can be reached. Such an understanding need not be consensual; it may be a source of conflict and controversy. It must nevertheless find at least partial validation in experience. Without the will, the understanding, and the validation, this reason to restrict free trade and qualify the doctrine of comparative advantage loses its force; no distance is a striking distance if there is no readily available and understood way of closing this distance.

A particular combination of features of the world economy today drastically expands the range of circumstances in which a relatively more backward economy may be able to enter repeatedly into lines of business in which a relatively more advanced one specializes—the situation of relative advantage. Multinational firms carry high-technology and avant-garde practices of production throughout the world, although they do so under the restraints imposed by the law of intellectual property. Governments in several major developing countries support advanced scientific and technological education and research. Yet the countries touched by such public and private initiatives often continue to sustain wage levels that are very low in comparison to those experienced in the richer economies. Wage levels may thus cease to be closely related to levels of labor productivity in the most advanced sectors of different national economies. In so doing, their power to influence the worldwide assignment of productive specializations among countries may weaken.

The cumulative result may be drastically to expand the number of economies, or of sectors of production in those economies, that come within striking range of each other. In this way, the thesis of relative advantage becomes applicable to a far broader range of situations than may at first have seemed to lie within its scope. From having seemed a marginal exception, the conjecture begins to look like an idea of wide if not pervasive relevance to the world economy. The further reaches of the spectrum at which it fails to apply—the circumstances of comparable or of very unequal levels of development—might then just as well be treated as the exceptions.

This thesis of relative advantage makes a prediction contrasting with many familiar arguments about the circumstances in which selective restraints on trade may be justified. The prediction is that in the condition of limited relative backwardness—the circumstance of the striking distance—it is the relatively backward rather than the relatively more advanced economy that will face the greatest dangers and have the strongest reason to impose such selective restraints.

The traditional reason to suppose that the burden falls chiefly on the relatively more advanced economy is that this economy might be expected to suffer the greatest loss of jobs, in competitive lines of business, to the economy that succeeds in making its cheaper labor in those same lines of business as productive as the labor of its relatively more advanced competitor. Within the way of thinking I here propose, this view requires two sets of corrections. The combined effect of these corrections is to invert the prediction of where the main burden is likely to fall.

The first correction is to insist that the view I resist exaggerates the benefits and underestimates the perils of reliance on cheaper labor. Upward pressure on returns to labor, and thus on the progressive replacement of resource-saving technologies and production processes by labor-saving technologies and production process, has always exerted a vital influence on economic growth. It has done so at every turning in the economic history of the modern world. Indeed, it played a part in accounting for the revolutionary economic advances that took place in the North Atlantic world from the late eighteenth century on.

The second correction is that the approach I reject fails to capture the task that is paramount in the circumstance of the striking distance: the need to experiment, and therefore to make mistakes and incur costs, in the early steps of action undertaken under the banner of the maxim that to imitate is to invent.

Underlying both corrections is an idea of more general application. To grasp a basic element in the dynamic of innovation and growth, think once again of a man and a machine. The man performs some actions that he does not yet know how to repeat and others that he does. As soon as he learns to repeat them he embodies the repetition in a formula, and the formula in a machine. His strategy is constantly to shift the focus of his attention and the use of his time from the repetitious to the not yet repeatable. Competitive pressure to replace the saving of resources by the saving of work will in time and overall be more of a boon than a bane because it will hasten this process.

What will happen if practices of benchmarking, imitation, and innovation suffer chill or disruption under the shadow of the overwhelming advantages (save for more expensive labor) enjoyed by a relatively more advanced trading partner? The result may be to interrupt, delay, or slow the changes (especially through the substitution of machines for repeatable labor and through the devotion of more time to the not yet formulaic) that make possible continuing rises in total factor productivity as well as in the productivity of labor. The prospect of such a misadventure supplies a major reason to accept restraints on trade in the situation of relative advantage.

The objection may be raised that under globalization, the discouragement to imitative innovation in the situation of relative advantage will lose much of its force, thanks to the ubiquity of multinational firms. Like bees pollinating one plant after another, such firms may be readily attracted to produce in the relatively backward economy, bringing with them the more advanced technologies of which they are the masters.

Three facts, however, combine greatly to diminish the value of this compensating consideration. The first fact is that the multinationals are likely to be attracted by significantly and enduringly lower labor costs. The preference for labor-saving technologies and for an upward tilt to the wage is, however, one of the concerns underlying the argument of this thesis. The second fact is that the multinationals have often preferred to produce, in such circumstances of cheaper labor, with relatively more backward technologies and more rigid production processes. Moreover, they have decomposed the process of production, locating the production of each input where it suits them. In both ways they have revealed their lack of a stake in the advance of the relatively more backward economy, through emulation and innovation, to the front line of world production. The third fact is that the gifts of the multinationals may come poisoned: they may inhibit the adaptation and development by the host country of the technologies they bring with them. The rules of intellectual property may aggravate the imported evil, adding to the seductions of greed the prohibitions of law. My earlier discussion of the economic significance of the political partition of humanity has suggested, and my later discussion of the thesis of self-revision will further explore, a basic economic reason for prizing national independence and divergence in the forms, directions, and uses of innovation.

Consider now the relation of the thesis of relative advantage to the traditional infant-industry argument in favor of selective protection. The thesis seeks to salvage and to rectify the element of distorted and truncated truth in this argument. However, it differs from the classic case for the protection of infant industries in two respects, one having to do with the infancy and the other with the industry.

For one thing, the emphasis of this conjecture is not on the early steps in incipient industries; it is on innovative procedures within industries that may have been long established and are located in countries that are now closing in on the trading partners with whom they have or contemplate free trade. This emphasis accords with a historical record in which countries that had already become major industrial powers, such as the United States of the late nineteenth and early twentieth centuries, combined sustained trade protection with high economic growth.

For another thing, the focus of this proposition addresses the whole of a national economy rather than particular firms, industries, or sectors. The hypothesis underlying this focus is that a relatively backward sector within a relatively advanced economy is likely to find itself in a fundamentally different situation from a relatively backward sector within a relatively backward economy. In the former instance, if talent and insight are at hand, the relatively backward sector will soon be able to draw in people, practices, technologies, and ideas from other sectors in the same, relatively advanced economy. It will benefit from all the physical, educational, and social capital that makes an advanced economy advanced. If, under such circumstances, talent and insight fail to compensate for the setback by mobilizing the physical, financial, human, and conceptual resources of neighboring sectors, no protectionist maneuver will rescue it from its self-inflicted failure. The standard case for free trade will apply. It is better to speak of outmatched economies than of infant industries.

The thesis of relative advantage gives rise to a complication in the design of a world trade regime that the related infant-industry argument, with its emphasis on sectors of an economy rather than on national economies as a whole, could never produce. If free trade is more justified between countries that are either comparably developed or very unequally developed, and less justified when the laggard can soon close in, by identifiable and feasible steps, on the leader, how could there ever be a set of universal trade rules that would serve the interests of all?

Those in the first situation would have reason to prefer trade that was as free as possible (subject to the vital qualifications suggested by the two theses that remain to be discussed). Those in the second situation would be better served (subject to the same qualifications) by a trading system that allowed them space to maneuver. Moreover, the relative positions of the trading partners would be forever changing, with the result that the global regime best at one time would not be best at another.

The central implication for the organization of the world trading system is that it must be designed, so far as is possible, to accommodate this wide diversity of interest and purpose. It must see such an accommodation not as a constraint but as a goal. It must place the value of experiment where the dogma of an imposed uniformity now sits.

I now take up four objections to the thesis of relative advantage. Discussion of them provides an opportunity to qualify the thesis of relative advantage in some respects while refining and radicalizing it in other ways. It is impossible to answer the objections without placing the thesis in the context of ideas about the world division of labor as well as about the method of economics.

A first objection is the absence of any uncontroversial metric by which to measure whether one national economy is within striking distance of another. Indeed, there is no such metric. The sense of the striking distance is pragmatic: whether there is a feasible series of steps—feasible for governments, firms, and other social and economic agents—that would enable workers and businesses to produce at comparable or lower cost the kinds of goods and services that a trading partner produces.

The trading partner need not produce exactly the same goods and services—tractors instead of cars, for example, or data collection and analysis for insurance companies instead of customer services for financial intermediaries. There will always be a large element of historical contingency or path dependence in any particular set of international economic specializations, given the advantages of scale, the benefits of clustering, and the value of accumulating and concentrating requisite skills. However, the outcome of the feasible convergence in capacities of production must be the production of goods and services that are analogous to those produced by the trading partner. Once again, the relevant test of analogy will be practical: how you can use one thing to do something else, or convert a particular skill into another one.

A hallmark of economic development is the ever larger role that will be played in an economy by generic capabilities. Of these, the most important are social and mental. They have to do with the mastery of innovation-friendly practices of cooperation and the redirection of time away from repeatable operations— embodied in machines—and toward those activities we do not yet know how to repeat. The more that economic life comes to be marked by these attributes, the greater becomes our power to use one thing to do something else and to convert a particular skill into another one. At higher levels of development, international specializations can therefore be expected to become more fluid. The barriers to entry into an analogous line of production will, other things equal, be less daunting.

Whether a national economy comes within striking distance of a trading partner will consequently depend on all the circumstances that may help or hinder the power of its governments and firms to escape the established worldwide distribution of comparative advantage and to build new comparative advantage. A country can increase this power by raising a shield over national heresy in its strategy of development so as to diminish its dependence on the interests and prejudices of foreign capital, foreign power, and foreign advice. To this end, it may need to mobilize its natural, financial, and human resources, up to the point of organizing a war economy without a war. It may need to create capabilities for the development or adaptation of technology that are not under the control of the dominant economic powers or of the multinational businesses associated with them. It may need to bring about a forced rise in its level of domestic saving (in conformity to the principle that foreign capital is the more useful the less it is required) and to develop new arrangements tightening the links between saving and investment. And it may need to subordinate the free flow of capital to the imperatives of its growth strategy. Defiance will not guarantee success. However, conformity, in all but the most special and transitory circumstances, is sure to spell failure.

The absence of any metric by which to measure the striking distance among national economies is closely related to two deep features of our experience and knowledge of society. The first such characteristic of social facts is the nonexistence of any closed space of possibilities. There is no antecedent list of possible states of affairs and no set of causal laws underwriting such a closure. The possible is the adjacent possible: the state of affairs that we can reach from where we are, by a series of next steps, with the institutional and conceptual materials at hand, enlarged by our halting powers of invention.

A second attribute of social facts has to do with the way in which they differ from natural facts. They do not exist univocally, as do objects in nature. They exist more or less, with greater or lesser degrees of entrenchment. It is to them, rather than to natural facts, that Aristotle's doctrine of degrees of being best applies. To the extent that the arrangements of society and the routines of culture, including our economic institutions and assumptions, are organized to set themselves beyond challenge, they present themselves falsely as natural objects. Relations among people appear, as Karl Marx argued in his criticism of political economy and of its "fetishism of commodities," as if they were relations of people to things.

We are not condemned to naturalize social facts, or to acquiesce in an organization of society and culture that enables them to wear the deceptive halo of naturalness and necessity. Our most powerful material, social, and spiritual interests are engaged in a reorganization of society and culture that strengthens our power to revise arrangements and assumptions without needing crisis as the condition of change.

According to a second objection, relative advantage is exceptional rather than commonplace. It would be a mistake, according to this complaint, to base our thinking about free trade on the anomalous rather than on the typical.

To understand why this objection is misguided, we should begin by recalling the most important implications of increasing returns to scale in comparative advantage. One implication is that the assignment of international specializations will have a large element of arbitrariness. Either of two trading partners at comparable levels of development might produce computers or airplanes. However, once one of the trading partners has achieved economies of scale and concentrations of skill in one of these lines of production rather than in another, its position may become relatively entrenched. A swap of lines of production between the trading partners may be difficult, even all but impossible, to accomplish.

Another implication is that advances in free trade may fail to be Pareto-improving: some participants in the trading regime may stand to lose.

The result is to make the particular content of any given distribution of productive specializations in the world if not arbitrary at least heavily dependent on particular, contingent sequences of events: which trading partner first achieves economies of scale and concentrations of skill in any given line of work. It may seem at first that this widening of the room for maneuver applies with full force only if the trading partners are at comparable levels of development. Substantial inequalities in technology and in total factor productivity might seem to preclude this result; businesses in the less technologically developed and productive economy may find it hard to gain entry to the lines of production that flourish in the relatively more advanced economy unless they manage to raise themselves far above the average level of technological and organizational refinement prevailing in their own national economy. By this reasoning, the thesis of relative advantage would indeed address an exceptional circumstance.

However, it does not apply merely to an exceptional circumstance. It applies more broadly, at the present time, for a reason that may seem largely circumstantial. This circumstantial reason turns out to be the contemporary expression of more lasting and universal forces.

The seemingly circumstantial reason is that the spread of advanced technologies and practices of production has come to coexist with vast disparities in the rewards of labor. As a result, many firms and whole sectors of production in some of the major developing countries can combine relatively low returns to labor with relatively high levels of labor productivity. More than any other fact, this combination helps widen the scope of the circumstances to which the thesis of relative advantage applies.

The diffusion of technologies is spurred by many different features of the contemporary situation. Among them are the global activities of multinational businesses, carrying machines and skills from one place to another, even when nothing but short-sighted greed drives them; the wavering attempts by national governments to develop technologies not under the control of the multinationals; and, above all, the power of education and emulation to develop and spread in ways that neither the profit-maximizing impulse nor the intellectual-property regime can control.

The persistence of relatively low returns to labor, even in countries and in businesses that have made dramatic advances in the productivity of labor, can be attributed to a single dramatic reality, the release of hundreds of million Chinese and Indian workers into what has become a world labor pool: one shaped by the denial to labor of the right to cross national frontiers. No wonder China and India have become the chief protagonists and beneficiaries of the circumstance that the thesis of relative advantage addresses.

We should recognize in each of the elements of this circumstance a foreshadowing of forces that are likely to outlast it and to deepen its effects. Imagine that many major developing countries succeeded in raising a shield over heresy in their strategies of national development and in mobilizing their natural, financial, and human resources. Imagine that this success allowed them to refuse the invitation to a slow, obedient ascent up the rungs of a predictable ladder of economic evolution. Imagine that the favored form of the division of labor, having ceased to be Adam Smith's pin factory, with its stark hierarchies and rigid specializations, increasingly became one in which the contrasts among all specialized roles as well as between roles of supervision and of execution weakened in the interest of permanent innovation. Imagine that this shift touched ever broader parts of each major national economy, not just the advanced sectors of high technology and deep knowledge. Imagine that all over the world we came increasingly to see production not only as the application of science but as a species of practical scientific experimentation: we understand by imagining transformative variation, and turn some of these imagined variations into things—goods and services for sale. Imagine persistent upward pressure on the wage to use machines as replacements for the operations we know how to repeat rather than to use people as replacements for the machines we do not yet find it worthwhile to buy or to develop. Imagine that the reorganization of education, of politics, and of culture all encouraged the radicalization of an experimentalist impulse, lessening the dependence of change on crisis. Imagine that the spread of scientific, technological, and organizational ideas and practices in the world continued, now inflamed by national commitments to rebel and to rise. And imagine that all these tendencies operated in a world that continued to restrict the mobility of labor and that, in part for that reason, continued as well to suffer vast inequalities among the living standards of different peoples.

In such a world, in which the persistence of global inequality and national sovereignty coexisted with the worldwide advance of experimentalist methods, attitudes, and arrangements, relative advantage would be recognized as the normal situation among trading partners. By contrast, trade among countries at either very unequal or roughly comparable levels of development would be regarded as precarious limiting cases. Businesses in poor countries, with poorly paid labor, could excel in advanced forms of production. Businesses in rich countries that enjoy high productivity of labor might suddenly falter in their success in conforming to the experimentalist imperative, or they might suffer the consequences of national failures to reorganize education and politics.

These imaginary suppositions are not so imaginary after all. They exaggerate and project tendencies that are among the most powerful at work in contemporary economies. By so doing, these suppositions help show why relative advantage can describe a common rather than an exceptional situation—today and in the future, so long as the world continues to be both economically unequal and politically divided.

A third objection is that the thesis of relative advantage reverses, without adequate justification, the emphasis of where free trade is likely to prove most troublesome. We are today more familiar with debate over the trouble that free trade may cause to workers and firms in the richer countries. The thesis, however, focuses in the first instance on the troubles that free trade may cause to the developing countries: those that come from below to enter the zone of the striking distance.

Before considering the deeper reason for the reversal of emphasis, it helps to begin by remembering the history of this debate. In
the nineteenth and the early twentieth centuries, the critics of free
trade had the same focus on the relatively backward rather than on
the relatively advanced economies. Such was the case, for example,
with the architects and theorists of the "American System," in
almost unbroken tradition from Alexander Hamilton to the New
Deal, as well as with Friedrich List and his German school of economic nationalism.

The contemporary association of trouble in the wake of free
trade with richer rather than poorer countries results from the
contingent combination of a theoretical bias with a political fact.
The theoretical bias is the inordinate influence that a particular
image of world trade has had on the development of trade theory
as well as on the course of practical policy debate ever since
Ricardo first proposed the doctrine of comparative advantage: the
image of capital-rich countries trading with labor-rich countries.
This image—I argued in the note at the end of the chapter on
comparative advantage—does ever less justice to the reality of
world trade. The political bias is the hold that the rich countries,
and their journals and universities, have over the main direction
of contests over policy.

The thesis of relative advantage predicts trouble in the relatively more advanced economy as well as in the relatively more
backward one. That attention, however, should fall in the first instance on the latter rather than on the former is a preference justified by a crucial difference between the two situations.

In the relatively more advanced economy it will in principle be
possible to compensate workers and firms for the loss imposed on
them by freer trade with the relatively more backward economy.
To be sure, if we take solely the analysis of static comparative advantage into account, there may be a loss to the relatively more
advanced economy as a whole as well as to particular firms and
workers within it. The loss to the society as a whole may result
from the damage done by freer trade to an entrenched position
that the relatively more advanced economy had achieved in particular lines of production, thanks to accumulations of scale and

skill. Susceptibility to such an event results from the implications of increasing returns to scale, in accordance with the way of thinking introduced by strategic trade theory.

If such a loss from trade were the end of the story, the theoretical possibility of compensating the losers from free trade for their loss would be of limited significance. The compensation would be unlikely to be given in fact: new slices would probably not be cut from a shrinking pie. In addition to being impractical, the compensatory possibility is also unpromising: it fails to suggest any distinctive advantage that may be enjoyed by a relatively more advanced economy, in contrast to a relatively more backward one, when faced with loss resulting from freer trade. However, the story does not end here.

Once we extend our view, from static efficiency to opportunities for development, we see that, in the circumstances characteristic of a relatively more advanced economy, such a trade loss can elicit a response, turning short-term loss into long-term gain. The erosion of the entrenched position may invite governmental, social, and private initiatives enlarging the role of the activities people do not yet know how to repeat, broadening access to the opportunities and resources of production for more economic agents on more terms, and forming, in the school, the firm, and the polity, the individual who is capable of devoting less of his time to compulsion and repetition. Nothing guarantees such a creative response to trouble. Nevertheless, something of the ability so to respond forms part of what makes an economy relatively more advanced in the first place.

Under the conditions of such a response, the power to compensate the losers for loss inflicted by freer trade will no longer be idle speculation. Retrospectively, the society will be richer and, with an expanding pie, better able to compensate the losers. Prospectively, the development of compensatory practices will form an important part of the struggle to prevent distributive conflict—the conflict, within the relatively more advanced economy, between losers and winners from freer trade—from inhibiting innovation as well as from discouraging commerce.

In the circumstances of the relatively more backward economy, loss from freer trade will present itself in a different key, with fewer resources and opportunities to respond through compensation, innovation, and reconstruction. There may be losers from freer trade. For example, farmers in the relatively more backward economy may be unable to survive competition with the more productive farmers of the relatively more advanced economy. In principle, these losers might be compensated, just as in the relatively more advanced economy, although the more backward economy will have fewer resources with which to compensate them.

However, there will not, even in principle, be a way of compensating the most important form of loss, the form that is especially significant for the thesis of relative advantage. This loss is the inhibition of a change: the entrance of firms and workers in the emerging economy into lines of production in which the relatively more advanced economy enjoys an entrenched position. These losers cannot even in principle be compensated for the simple reason that they do not yet exist. They are potential, not existing, economic agents.

This difference in the ability to compensate is the shallow expression of a deeper distinction. A characteristic feature of economic development is the facility of shifting from one line of economic activity to another, from one set of products to another, from one set of inputs to another, from one set of machines to another. This plasticity has multiple roots. Of these roots, three are preeminent.

The first root is the development of human capital: the number of people with the educational equipment to master a core of generic conceptual and practical capabilities. This mastery prepares them to play roles in the dialectic between the repeatable, embodied in formulas and in machines, and the not yet repeatable, the concern of the forward edge of production.

A form of education that is oriented to analysis and problem solving rather than to information, that is therefore more interested in selective penetration than in encyclopedic coverage, that advances by contrast of methods and ideas rather than by worship of a single canon of belief and intellectual practice, and that is cooperative rather than individualist or authoritarian will contribute powerfully to this result. It will help each individual worker and citizen think and act as the context-transcending subject that he really is rather than as a zombie acting out someone else's script. For one society to be relatively more developed than another means, in part, for it to have more people with such powers.

The second root is the spread of a family of innovation-friendly practices of cooperation. Economic and technological progress, I have argued, requires both innovation and cooperation. Innovation, whether technological or organizational, depends on cooperation: it is only by cooperating that people can introduce and deploy a novel technology or a new way of working together. Any innovation, however, threatens to disturb the vested rights and settled expectations in which every cooperative regime is embedded. The reason is that an innovation will always seem more useful or more threatening to some of the groups that participate in that regime than to others. A mechanical invention, for example, may seem to threaten the employment of one group of workers in an industry while increasing opportunities for another group.

Practices that moderate, although they cannot extinguish, the tension between cooperation and innovation play a major part in every aspect of the material advance of humanity, including economic growth and technological innovation. Certain attributes of society and culture promote this family of practices: the avoidances of rigid and entrenched rankings of class and caste that restrict the way in which people can work together and use machines; the society-wide grant of basic educational and economic endowments, made independent not only of occupying any particular station in society but also of holding any particular job in the production system; and the strengthening of an experimentalist impulse in culture. To give a larger place to the practices of innovation-friendly cooperation than another society does forms part of what makes that society more developed than another. One of the telling and important consequences of this advantage will be a greater power to reorient and reorganize production in the face of the opportunities and dangers presented by freer trade.

It is never an advantage possessed and maintained in tranquility. At any moment, distributive conflict over the costs and benefits of innovation may overwhelm this advantage in even the richest economies and the most educated societies. We can moderate the tension between innovation and cooperation. We cannot abolish it.

A third source of this plasticity has to do with the consequences of relations among productive activities in the relatively more advanced economy. In this economy, there will be denser clusters of firms and networks of production. The distinctions among lines of production will be less rigid, and the opportunity to use the skills, technologies, and practices deployed in one field to produce goods or services in a neighboring field will be more ample.

These powers do not result solely from the quantity of productive activity in the relatively more advanced economy; they result as well from its quality. As an economy develops, conceptual operations, especially conceptual operations combining repetitious and not yet repeatable elements, play an increasing role. So does a form of the division of labor very different from Adam Smith's pin factory, one that softens the contrasts between the formulation and the execution of productive tasks as well as among specialized jobs in a process of production. There will be a repertory of productive capabilities more susceptible to being extracted from their present uses and turned to other uses.

Given the combination of quantitative density and qualitative abstraction or generality in the production system of the more advanced economy, it is likely to be easier than it would be, under conditions of less density and less generality, to turn one line of production into another: to move from the production of a good and service to some feasible next step or substitute, deploying, with a difference, capabilities, practices, and technologies that have already been acquired and mastered.

A foreseeable effect of these features of production in the more advanced economy is that its entrepreneurs and businesses will enjoy greater ability to respond to the competitive pressure of freer trade by moving resources, people, and skills from one line of production to the next. To make the existing networks of production and clusters of firms yet denser, thanks to analogical extensions or combinations, will be the predictable response of the more developed economy to such pressure. Part of what it means for an economy to be more advanced is that it enjoys, in higher measure, this facility for substitution in the face of competition.

The relatively less developed economy will be far more hamstrung, with respect to this third source of plasticity as well as with regard to the other two sources. Its firms, entrepreneurs, and workers will be less able to compete with firms, entrepreneurs, and workers that can draw on all the powers defining the circumstance of greater development: more people with generic capabilities, more groups adept at innovation-friendly cooperation, more firms and government agencies able to respond to competition in trade through the analogical extension and reconstruction of established practices and lines of production.

The temptation to respond to this disadvantage by maintaining downward pressure on the wage may then prove an ambiguous benefit. The wage bill is likely to represent a limited and decreasing part of the costs of production in many sectors of a contemporary economy. Moreover, the absence of upward pressure on the wage may discourage rather than facilitate the attempt to enhance the productivity of labor and to arouse permanent organizational and technological innovation.

No real and robust symmetry exists between the conditions in which the relatively more advanced and the relatively more backward economy encounter the troubles of free trade when the latter is within striking distance of the former; thus the emphasis of the thesis of relative advantage on the backward economy as a potential loser rather than on potential losers within the advanced economy.

There is what may at first appear to be a major exception to the idea that, in the situation of relative advantage, the burden is likely to fall more heavily on the advanced economy than on the backward one. The exception is the relation of China to the rest of the world economy and especially to the rich countries at the time of the publication of this book. In many lines of production, China has come within striking distance of the more advanced economies. It has sometimes overtaken them. Each successive move in the opening of the Chinese economy seems to be accompanied by China's winning of more market share in more of the sectors of production in which some of its trading partners had seemingly entrenched positions. Freer trade, under relative advantage, appears to have brought this most important contemporary developing country one success after another.

With this China as the most visible contemporary instance of the relation between more advanced and more backward economies under a regime of free trade, the practical debate about free trade seems to have been turned upside down. In the nineteenth and early twentieth centuries, resistance to free trade was characteristic of emerging economies, like the United States. Enthusiastic adherence to free trade was a mark of the pioneering industrial and commercial power, Great Britain, or of much poorer economies with much less favored place in the international division of labor, like many of the Latin American countries. Now free trade has come to be feared in some of the leading economic powers, and the greatest focus of this fear has been their trading relation to China. Consider, in the light of ideas introduced earlier in this book, the meaning of this reversal and its significance for the thesis of relative advantage.

China's place in the world economy during this period exemplified a special combination of circumstances. This combination may (as I suggested earlier in discussing the consequences of the combination of sustained wage repression with greater access to worldwide technologies of production) lengthen the striking distance invoked by the thesis of relative advantage. In many sectors, an economy may, given these conditions, come within striking distance of another one even as it remains much poorer.

When pushed to the hilt, as it has been in China, the same combination of circumstances may also reassign, for a while, the risks and burdens with which the thesis of relative advantage deals. It may allow an emerging economy to create a limited disturbance for its richer trading partners. The trade that begins by threatening unskilled laborers may end up threatening ever more skilled, white-collar or blue-collar workers as the rising economy enters more advanced sectors of production.

The threat from abroad works by reinforcing other, more power-ful forces internal to the economies and to the politics of the richer countries. These forces weaken the position of labor in relation to capital. They may be, in the first instance, technological develop-ments, but they are always, in the final instance, political defeats. Technology is indeterminate in its distributive consequences; what matters is the institutional setting in which it operates. In many of the advanced Western societies, this institutional setting has be-come increasingly unfavorable to labor. The Left has failed to rein-vent its programmatic direction and to rebuild its social base. In the absence of such a reinvention and rebuilding, the vested rights of workers in traditional mass-production industries have often come to seem both unaffordable and unjust, because enjoyed at the cost of other, less privileged workers as well as of consumers.

The victims of these events in the richer countries may be de-nied the benefit of policies of social insurance, of economic recon-struction and retraining, and of the broadening of economic and educational opportunity that only institutional change, forged in the struggle over the mastery and uses of state power, can ulti-mately achieve. This is a real, not a sham, problem. However, it is different in character, and more limited in scope, than the danger that plays the central role in the thesis of relative advantage: the in-hibition to national development, to economic growth, especially as achieved by permanent revolution in productivity.

Only if a more advanced economy were to fail dramatically in responding to change in the international division of labor by de-veloping new comparative or absolute advantage to replace the advantages of which it had been deprived would its troubles then become more substantial. Only then would these troubles resem-ble the difficulties on which the thesis of relative advantage fo-cuses. Such more formidable difficulties are evident in China's contemporary relations to a range of middle-income countries that have failed to sustain gains in either total factor or labor pro-ductivity but that have continued to guarantee a much higher wage than Chinese firms pay their workers.

To appreciate the significance of the Chinese experience for the thesis of relative advantage, it is necessary to understand China's unique variation on the circumstances—common in the world today—that may enable an emergent economic power to extend its striking distance within the international division of labor.

On the one hand, China witnessed severe and persistent containment of labor costs. This wage repression only recently began to weaken. Hundreds of millions of former peasants or their children were driven from agriculture to industry—a "reserve labor army" if there ever was one. This was a one-time event of vast consequence. In the larger setting of world history, however, it represented less an anomaly than an extreme instance of a familiar event. Such dislocations had taken place, and continued to occur, on a smaller scale, elsewhere. On the other hand, China experienced ongoing rises in productivity (especially labor productivity, as distinguished from total factor productivity) in particular sectors of the economy, secured in the context of radical and growing inequality among sectors of the economy, as well as among regions of the country and classes of society.

What allowed the repression of monetary and nonmonetary returns to labor to coexist with continued, sector-specific rises in productivity, resulting in low unit-labor costs, was the marriage of inequality with dictatorship: dictatorship in culture and social life as well as in politics. Not only was the nation disenfranchised and deprived of a voice, it was also denied the means—in politics, in public discourse, and in ordinary consciousness—to define alternative national futures, to debate them, and to implement them.

The alliance of inequality with dictatorship shaped China's spectacular if unequal growth. It shaped it, however, in combination with a strategy of national development that defied the global economic orthodoxy of the time. That strategy disobeyed this orthodoxy in two respects.

The first respect was its insistence on raising what I earlier called a shield over heresy. China based its development on the mobilization of its own human, financial, and natural resources rather than on foreign capital. It resisted deep foreign penetration of its economy. It avoided the initiatives—common, for example in Latin America at the time—that would it have put it at the mercy of the interests and prescriptions of the dominant powers.

The second respect was the fecundity of China's institutional innovations in its ways of organizing market-oriented economic activity and of relating governmental initiative to private enterprise. The failure to democratize either politics or culture, however, decisively compromised the reach and the integrity of such innovations. The institutional experiments were truncated rather than deepened. As a result, they could not help sustain continued gains in total factor productivity or inform a long-term strategy of economic growth.*

The organization of the country resulting from these facts did not prevent technologies of production established in the rich countries from being imitated, adapted, and deployed in particular sectors of the Chinese economy. However, it did stifle China's collective capacity for self-transformation in the workplace, the school, the firm, or the state and society as whole. It is a capacity as indispensable to continuing economic progress as to every other form of social empowerment. For this reason, we should see the Chinese exception less as an omen of the future—for the world or for China itself—than as a limited success, bought at a terrible price.

A fourth objection to the thesis of relative advantage is that by focusing on whole national economies rather than on particular businesses, the thesis of relative advantage makes the common mistake, anathema to the theory of international trade, that countries can compete. According to the objection, only firms or particular economic agents can compete in the sense of competition that is pertinent to trade theory. Refutation of this criticism provides an opportunity to connect the statement of the thesis of relative advantage with my earlier discussion of comparative advantage. So long as the political partition of humanity persists, countries—or

*For a discussion of the importance of China's arrested institutional innovations to an understanding of national alternatives and alternative globalizations, see my book, *Democracy Realized: The Progressive Alternative,* Verso, 1998, pp. 105–112; and, with Zhiyuan Cui, "China in the Russian Mirror," *New Left Review,* I/208, November-December 1994, pp. 78–87.

the regional unions or empires into which they may organize themselves—remain the major sites for the making of comparative advantage as well as for the deepening of economic diversity: diversity of products and forms of production, of arrangements, practices, and beliefs. Less diversity means less interesting stuff on which the mechanisms of competitive efficiency can operate, to the detriment of the whole world as well as of each of its peoples.

In the narrow and dominant tradition of economic analysis, only firms can compete; the idea of competition among countries is dismissed as a misuse based on a misunderstanding. Even the ancient infant-industry argument for protection singles out particular businesses or sectors rather than whole national economies. In the broader historical study of modern economies and polities, however, capitalism has been recognized to be the brother of nationalism; trade, the cousin of empire; and the creation of wealth, within and beyond national borders, the ward of political protection. Where, between these two perspectives, does the thesis of relative advantage fit, with its emphasis on the inhibitions of free trade between countries at moderately unequal levels of development and productivity?

The powers by which comparative advantage can be made or reshaped transcend the firm. Even when they operate through the firm, they do not originate in particular businesses. Among these powers are the three sources of facility to substitute one line of production or one form of production for another that I discussed in responding to the previous objection: the development of individuals with generic conceptual and practical capabilities, the diffusion of practices of innovation-friendly cooperation, and the facility to carry skills, practices, and technologies from one line of production to another, responding to competition through substitution or reorientation.

Consider, for example, the third of these powers. Of the three, it is the one whose location beyond the level of the firm may seem least obvious; it is relatively more plain that the firms themselves cannot guarantee either education in generic capabilities or the conditions that I earlier described as conducive to the vigor and spread of innovation-friendly cooperation. The less dense the network of firms and lines of production (quantitative rarefaction) and the less advanced they are in using skills, technologies, and practices that can be readily disembedded from their present uses (qualitative embeddedness), the greater will be the need for some form of collective action or governmental initiative to make up for the relative weakness. Society and the state will have to supply the missing links: technologies that meet the next productive task while taking best advantage of established skills and available resources, forms of technical education that make up for the absence of pertinent traditions of craft, arrangements for the pooling of resources that quicken and cheapen the achievement of economies of scale. The provision of these missing links, which we might describe as quasi-public goods, strengthens the power of firms to respond, through analogy and substitution, to competitive pressure and opportunity.

The provision of the missing links may need to be organized by some form of cooperative competition among firms or communities. Or it may require to be established as well by the government, working with firms and communities to develop a distinct form of industrial policy: one that, instead of supporting certain sectors of the economy to the detriment of others, seeks to make up for the circumstances of relative backwardness (resulting in what I called rarefaction and embeddedness) that inhibit the power to move from one line of production and from one set of skills to the next.

Such initiatives do not make one national economy more competitive than another in the sense in which one firm can produce a good or service more efficiently than another. They nevertheless represent a second-order level of competitive vigor. They enhance the vigor of an economy in the defense of established comparative advantage and in the construction of new comparative advantage. Moreover, they do so at a level that no analysis of the activity of the firm can adequately capture. The thesis of relative advantage deals with this crucial second order of effects.

The idea of second-order competitive effects deserves to be generalized. We cannot understand the realities and possibilities of worldwide trade by focusing solely on particular firms and producers as if national boundaries were merely accidental obstacles to an activity calculated to defy them. We should not think and speak as if, once having justified the distinction between trade among countries and market-oriented exchange within them, the distinctions among national societies then lost all further relevance to our understanding of the risks and benefits of international trade.

On the contrary, the distinct, politically organized societies in the world remain the most important sites of difference: difference in institutional arrangements and in forms of consciousness, informing difference in what is produced and in how it is produced. Difference is not only part of the problem of organizing a world division of labor helping lift from mankind the burdens of poverty, infirmity, and drudgery; it is also part of the solution to that problem. Without the creation of more difference, the selective machinery of worldwide trade, based on established or constructed comparative advantage, has less material on which to operate and less potential of benefit.

Until it is supplemented by a view of how difference is created, a theory of comparative efficiencies in production would be like the present-day form of Darwin's theory of evolution, cut in half: natural selection unaided by genetic variation. Without the form of difference resulting from the political partition of the world, the full weight of creating difference would need to be rendered internal to the organization of the economy: for example, by the adoption of arrangements facilitating, through coexistence of alternative regimes of contract and property, a radical pluralism and an ongoing reform of economic institutions.

In fixing on second-order competitive effects and inhibitions, the thesis of relative advantage looks beyond the narrow horizon of static comparative advantage to a world of real societies and economies in which people gain strength, or suffer restraint, in the power to create comparative advantage. Firms are not that world; they are only players within it and expressions of its characteristic capacities and infirmities.

The extent to which a particular business bears the imprint of a particular national economy, and of the society and culture of which it forms part, is nevertheless itself variable. We must understand and use this variation to develop alternatives to the present organization of market economies and of global trade.

On the one hand, the world economy is in the process of being reorganized as a network of advanced sectors of production, marked by the predominance of the practices of innovation-friendly cooperation as well as by accumulations of knowledge and technology. The communion of these advanced sectors throughout the world, often only tenuously linked to other sectors of their national economies, has become a commanding force in the international economy. A fateful question is thus presented to us. Shall we remain condemned to attenuate the inequalities and exclusions produced by the division between advanced and backward sectors of each national economy? And to attenuate them through the two traditional devices of state support for the diffusion of small-scale property and business and of governmental commitment to compensatory redistribution through tax or transfer? Or will we, instead, succeed in overcoming this division through governmental, social, and private initiatives that enable the accelerated experimentalism of the advanced sectors to flourish far beyond the boundaries of the limited social and economic terrain in which they have taken hold so far?

On the other hand, a sign of success in the generalization and radicalization of the experimentalist impulse will be that the individual and the firm will become less dependent on the limitations of the collective milieu in which they operate. Of all forms of innovation, the most fundamental is the capacity to transcend the context. Contexts, however, including national and international economic institutions, can differ in the extent to which they support and develop this capacity. Much of the dominant tradition of theorizing about trade speaks as if the power of the firm to transcend its national setting were a matter of course. It is a program rather than a premise.

The Thesis of Politics over Economics

The efficacy of restraints on trade depends on the recalcitrance of the state to capture by powerful interests as well as on the experimental character of trade policy. The most effective way to make the state less vulnerable to such interests over the long term is to make it more radically democratic.

Restraints on free trade may be desirable in the circumstance of relative advantage. However, although this circumstance may be a necessary requirement for restraints on trade to be justified, it is not a sufficient one. The desirability and the dangers of such restraints depend as well on the way that the state is organized and policy made and implemented. The restraints require selectivity in protection, and selectivity is an invitation to capture by powerful private interests as well as to the bureaucratic impulse to "pick winners" top down. Whether what seems best in principle—selective and strategic protection in the situation of relative advantage—will prove also to be best in practice may turn on the extent to which the organization of politics and of policy making escape the twin evils of favoritism and dogmatism.

An authoritarian and enlightened bureaucracy able to insulate itself from powerful interests may in the short run defeat the first evil, under special conditions and even then only for a while. It will never defeat the second. The solution is to deepen democracy rather than to limit it, and to make the formulation and implementation of policy, including trade policy, pluralistic, participatory, and experimental in temper as well as in procedure. Politics will again be not fate but anti-fate.

Restraints on free trade are most likely to be justified in the middle zone, the area of the striking distance, the situation of relative advantage. To lie within the situation of relative advantage, however, is not a sufficient basis for such restraints. Something else matters decisively: politics—the form of the state, of the struggle over power, and of the practices for making and implementing policy. The debate about free trade opens up, inescapably, to the question of how best to understand the relation between economics and politics: its relation in the states and economies that we might create with instruments and ideas at hand as well as in the economies and states that already exist.

Because restraints on trade embody the power of government intervening in economic life, they may become tools of two different evils: the evil of the capture of government by powerful, organized interests and the evil of the disorientation of government under the spell of influental, costly dogmas. To justify such restraints, it is not enough to appeal to the circumstance of relative advantage; it is necessary as well to show how they can be formulated and implemented in such a way that the burden of the twin evils will not annul their value.

The idea of the twin evils supports one of the most familiar lines of argument about any policy that, like restraints on trade, uses governmental power selectively to allocate rights and benefits. Every restraint on free trade will embody such selectivity. It will do so even in the limiting case of an all-inclusive tariff at a flat and universal rate. Such a tariff will prefer the interests of producers to those of consumers. Depending on the reactions of a country's trading partners, it will also prefer the interests of import-substituting industries to those of import-using industries. Selectivity will be the horse on which privilege and dogma can ride together.

This fact lends support to a style of argument that serves as the stock objection to every governmental initiative that appears to restrict or to trump a decision made by the market. The objection may be pertinent even if the initiative is calculated to reshape the market, the better to give more people access to more markets in more ways. Remember the example of rules and policies that by distributing land, by broadening access to agricultural credit and technology, by supporting networks of cooperative competition among family farmers, and by supplying antidotes to the economic and natural risks of agricultural production make feasible an agricultural economy of highly productive family farms. By allowing a country to avoid the model of agrarian concentration that Karl Marx found in the history of England and that he mistook for the irresistible logic of capitalism, such a regime may create a new type of agricultural market. Indeed, in nineteenth-century American history it did create one—the most efficient that had ever existed, up till then, in world history.

What may seem, when viewed statically, as a market-trumping intervention may appear, when considered dynamically, as part of a historical sequence, as a moment in the reconstruction of the market. Just as the way of thinking from which the argument of the twin evils arises acknowledges only a single, convergent institutional form of the state and of democratic politics, it sees only one institutional version of the market.

Thus arises the immensely influential idea that although an intervention in restraint of trade may in principle seem appealing, it will almost always in practice lack sufficient justification. It is the idea that whatever the theoretical advantages of selective economic policy, in particular the advantages of selective policy in restraint of trade, such advantages will in fact be undermined by the twin evils accompanying governmental intervention in the economy: the theoretical second best of unconditional adherence to free trade will turn out to be the practical first best.

The influence of this idea was manifest in the development of strategic trade theory in the 1970s and 1980s. The strategic trade theorists of the late twentieth century questioned many of the assumptions of free trade doctrine. They nevertheless stepped back from the theoretical as well as the practical implications of their own views. They feared being mistaken for defenders of protectionism, and cited in defense of their caution one or another version of the twin evils argument. This safeguard encouraged timidity in theorizing. Strategic trade theorists would have done better to understand and to represent their own proposals as points of departure for a questioning of more general ideas that had come to be established in economics.

They could not have worked out such implications, going far beyond the boundaries of trade theory, without confronting the assumptions and equivocations of the twin evils arguments. They failed to force such a confrontation. As a result, strategic trade theory repeated, in its own way and on its own scale, the downward trajectory of the development theory of the mid-twentieth century: by failing to exploit the subversive theoretical significance of its own concerns and tenets, it reduced itself to the condition of a satellite to the ways of thinking it had failed to challenge. It then nearly ceased to matter as an independent theoretical enterprise.

The hidden theoretical core of the twin evils argument is disbelief in our power to transform the basic ways in which states and economies can relate to each other; the selective use of govern-mental power, in trade policy as elsewhere, will inevitably sacrifice decentralized experiment to enthroned prejudice and allow the privileged and the influential to harness the authority of govern-ment to their own selfish interests. According to this outlook, markets will be markets and states will be states; we can no more reinvent the basic institutional forms and practical consequences of governmental intervention in the economy than we can re-make the institutional form of the market economy itself.

There is, however, a crucial asymmetry in the institutional dog-matism on which the twin evils argument rests. Markets will be markets, but, insofar as they are not marred by imperfections, they cure their own defects; as an instrument for resource alloca-tion and for the accommodation of competing interests, they amount, according to that way of thinking, to a perpetual-motion machine. States will be states, and insofar as they meddle in the procedures and outcomes of a market system that is imagined to have its own institutional logic and integrity, they will end up serving prejudice and privilege.

We soon discover that the twin evils argument is not merely about free trade, and the occasions on which trade may usefully be restrained; it is about two connected issues that hold great in-terest for an understanding of economic life. The first issue is the institutional form of the market and of the state and therefore also of the ways in which market and state can relate to each other. The second issue is the primacy of politics over economics: its primacy in shaping the institutions and the practices that de-fine the market economy, set the range of its alternative possible forms, and organize the process by which we can change these forms.

Economic activity is social activity. Nothing is more important to economic growth than the relation between cooperation and innovation; the best cooperative regime, from the standpoint of growth, will be the one that is most hospitable to innovation—in technologies, organizations, practices, and ideas. How we move toward this ideal is in the first instance an institutional question and a political one. This consideration alone would suffice to suggest the central importance to economic thinking of the two issues described in the previous paragraph.

I propose five conjectures in opposition to the assumptions of the twin evils argument. They provide elements of a way of thinking about free trade—and about much else—developing ideas introduced in the previous chapter.

The first hypothesis is that a market economy can take alternative institutional forms. There is no single system of contract and property that can rightly be said to be implicit in the idea of a market economy. There are alternative possible regimes of contract and property under which decentralized economic activity—with many different agents bargaining on their own initiative and for their own account—can be carried out.

The conception of a market economy presupposed in our ordinary economic and political thinking is internally complex. It includes elements that may be in tension with one another or that may take different forms: for example, the decentralization of economic decisions and the absolute character of the control that each economic agent enjoys over the resources at his command. The classical right of private property, as imagined in nineteenth-century legal and economic theory, afforded near absolute discretion to the owner: within the domain of his ownership, he could do with his property almost whatever he wanted, regardless of its effects on others. Similarly, the classical right of contract tried to distinguish clearly between the articulated and reciprocal bargain (the bilateral executory contract) that gave rise to contractual obligations and the subtle interdependencies of social life. Such interdependencies generate forms of reliance and of expectation that were denied legal consequence.

This regime of private law shielded the owner against both state and society. It sacrificed to this single, overpowering objective any interest in expanding the range of economic agents who could in fact exercise the powers of property or in changing, for the sake of such a broadening of access, the nature and scope of those powers. It subordinated the diffusion of property, and the collective and individual opportunity to experiment with the arrangements for exchange among economic agents, to the imposition of a single model of ownership. This was not the market economy. It was just one way of understanding and organizing a market economy, although it was the way that acquired exemplary status for economic theory.

We cannot map out prospectively a closed horizon of possible institutional forms of the market economy, or indeed of possible institutional forms of any other domain of social life. Alternatives develop—most often by analogical extension and recombination—from the existing forms, under the pressure of conflicting interests and visions. At any given moment, the repertory of established or available institutional arrangements is relatively inelastic, in the imagination as well as in practice. Our assumptions and attitudes about abstract institutional conceptions, like the market economy or representative democracies, are largely shaped by the particular forms that these abstractions have taken in our individual and collective experience.

The second hypothesis is that the same principle of the decisive importance of institutional variation must apply to the organization of the state and to the ways in which government may engage the market. It is misleading to bring this engagement under the loaded label of "governmental intervention in the market"; the label suggests that the market has a permanent and universal nature, which the state must either respect or disrespect. A government can regulate market behavior from a distance. It can redistribute, through taxation and transfers, the results of economic activity. It can also, however, act to alter the rules and practices defining the market economy. According to an idea invoked earlier, what statically may seem to be no more than a subsidy, trumping an allocation of resources determined by the market as it is now organized, may dynamically turn out to be a move in the reorganization of the market economy. It may even amount to a move that makes more opportunities of decentralized economic initiative available to more people in more ways.

The third hypothesis is that the burden of the twin evils—of dogmatism and favoritism—in the imposition of selective restraints on free trade, whether by tariff, by quota, or by other devices, is variable. The double burden varies according to the way the government, politics, and the implementation of policy are organized. The dangers invoked by the twin evils argument are not fanciful; they are real. However, they are neither universal nor constant, as the contrasting examples of Latin America and northeast Asia in the late twentieth century suggest.

A country that avoids a top-down, secretive, and authoritarian approach to the formulation of trade policy will be less prone to the evil of dogmatism than a country that prefers to formulate policy, including trade policy, in a consultative, participatory, pluralistic, and experimental manner. The organization of politics—if by politics we mean struggle over the use as well as over the mastery of governmental power—will be decisive in shaping the range of options in every branch of economic policy, including trade policy.

The fourth hypothesis is that a powerful, relatively isolated bureaucracy operating in the context of limited democracy and of an authoritarian political culture can best be understood, in the setting of the controversy over free trade, as a costly and perilous shortcut to the route of escape from the first of the twin evils, the evil of favoritism. A powerful bureaucracy, relatively free from entanglements with the national plutocracy and relatively immunized against the surprises of political pressure and electoral upheaval, may succeed for a while in formulating trade policy that is not simply beholden to narrow cliques of special interests. Such is the circumstance that in recent decades we associate most readily with the experience of the northeast Asian economies.

This independence, however, will be fragile. It will also be bought at high cost. In an unequal society, with limited democracy and little vibrant public debate, the bureaucratic apparatus responsible for making trade policy will find itself, in its relation to the plutocratic interests, in a position similar to the relation of the imperial authorities to the landowning magnates in the agrarian-bureaucratic empires that dominated so much of world history. The central administration may try to contain the voracity of those elites, but it cannot resist them too much without mobilizing as a broad-based coalition of popular interests (the peasantry and smallholders of the agrarian-bureaucratic empires, the workers and small-time or would-be entrepreneurs of today) as a counterweight.

The bureaucrats have reason to hesitate before arousing a force that they may prove unable to ride. The more unequal the society, the more isolated the bureaucratic apparatus must become if it is to preserve its independence from the most powerful organized interests, and the sharper the dilemma it will face in choosing between the risks of accommodation and of confrontation with those interests.

It may achieve some independence from them. However, it cannot achieve independence from its stake in the perpetuation of its own power. Moreover, the very devices through which it secures itself against imprisonment by the rent-seeking interests may increase the likelihood of its surrender to the temptations of imposed and ignorant dogma, deaf to the lessons of experience from below.

If the bureaucracy responsible for the making of policy operates in the setting of authoritarian politics and of a culture inimical to the radicalization of experimentalism, the shortcut will be even more dangerous. The danger of clinging to yesterday's success or of following today's fashion will increase, and the power to imagine alternatives, and to try them out successively or simultaneously, will diminish.

The twin evils argument has been colored and supported by the association of restraints on trade—and more generally of selective governmental interventions in the market—with these facts. However, it has drawn from them the wrong conclusions because it has mistakenly supposed them to be necessary and universal features of the relation between government and the economy. It has assumed that in this relation, one of two circumstances must always and everywhere hold. If there is no part of the state capable of resisting capture at least partially (for example, the relatively independent bureaucracies of the northeast Asian "tiger" economies of the second half of the twentieth century), the twin evils of favoritism and dogmatism will occur unabated. If there is such a part of the state, the first evil may be attenuated, but only at the cost of aggravating the second. Society will be at greater risk of weakening its power to experiment—the very power that represents the chief strength of the market economy.

The fifth hypothesis is that the sole alternative to the burdensome and menacing shortcut discussed by the fourth hypothesis is the deepening of democracy and the radicalization of experimentalism. Consider the character of the institutional requirements for the overcoming of each of the twin evils.

The only safe antidote to the evil of capture of government by privileged interests lies in the convergence of two distinct but connected sets of events: the attenuation of entrenched and extreme inequalities, of organization and influence as well as of income, wealth, and power, and the development of a high-energy democracy, one organized to heighten the level of sustained popular engagement in politics and to diminish the dependence of transformation on crisis. The more the institutions of society, especially its political institutions, are organized to multiply opportunities and instruments for the remaking of social arrangements, piece by piece and step by step, the less will major change, although undertaken in piecemeal manner, need to await trauma in the form of economic crisis or warfare. It would be necessary both to raise the temperature of politics (through arrangements that encourage an organized and sustained heightening of popular engagement in political life) and to quicken its pace (through arrangements that resolve impasse over policy quickly, if necessary by early elections or programmatic plebiscites). At the same time, this high-energy democracy would need to enhance the capability-supporting economic and educational endowments of the individual while making it easier for particular sectors or localities to try out countermodels to the prevailing national path. We cannot produce such effects without innovating in the very restricted repertory of institutional arrangements that now define representative democracy.*

*In other writings I have discussed the institutional content of changes in the organization of democratic politics that would make the state less likely to be captive to privileged interests and public policy less likely to serve as the handmaiden to dogma. See *False Necessity: Antinecessitarian Social Theory in the Service of Radical Democracy*, Verso, 2001, pp. 207–221, 441–476; *Democracy Realized: The Progressive Alternative*, Verso, 1998, pp. 191–197, 212–220, 261–277; *What Should the Left Propose?*, Verso, 2005, pp. 29–31, 156–163.

It is a route unmarked by any available institutional blueprint. Although it may, indeed it ordinarily must, be taken in small, accretive steps if it is to be taken at all, it is beset by many perils. The most immediate of these dangers, from the standpoint of the evil of capture of government by powerful special interests, is that things may get worse before they get better. A government that loses its bureaucratic and authoritarian hardness may, in the process of becoming more democratic, become more porous and pliant. It may become more susceptible to privileged interests before it recovers its resistance to them in the more durable forms produced by the raised temperature and the quickened pace of democratic politics.

To overcome the evil of dogmatism in turn requires an enlargement of the repertory of ways in which governments and firms may work together. The two institutional models for the relation between public authority and private enterprise now available in the world are the American model of the arm's length regulation of business by government and the northeast Asian model of unitary trade and industrial policy made and imposed, top down, by a central bureaucracy. Solving the problem of dogmatism, in trade as in other areas of economic policy, requires a different practice and a different vision: participation—broadly based and with the lights of public scrutiny turned on—rather than imposition, and pluralistic experiment instead of uniform dogma. Such an approach to the making and implementation of policy is likely to flourish only in the climate of deepened, high-energy democracy: hence the affinity between the institutional requirements for redressing each of the twin evils.

Even such a democracy may represent only part of the favorable background, the part that has to do with institutions. No less important is the part that has to do with consciousness, the forms of culture and education that, in every department of social life, break down barriers between the ordinary moves we make within an accepted framework of conduct or belief and the exceptional moves by which we challenge and change pieces of that framework.

What are the implications of these five hypotheses for our thinking about free trade and for our efforts to reshape the market economy and to direct the form and consequences of economic growth through political initiative? The thesis of relative advantage suggested that the benefits of free trade are likely to be most pronounced, and its dangers most limited, when the trading partners are either at comparable or at sharply different levels of economic development. The case for such restraints will be greatest in the middle zone in which, although the trading economies are unequally developed and productive, the relatively more backward one lies within striking distance of the relatively more advanced one.

The situation of relative advantage is a necessary but not a sufficient condition for the imposition of selective restraints on free trade. The benefits of such restraints, in that situation, will not outweigh their costs unless a state imposes them in a manner that contains or moderates the twin evils of preconception and collusion, of picking winners or of letting losers pick governments and direct their policies. The familiar way to contain or moderate these evils—through selective trade policy, made and implemented by an independent governmental apparatus able to insulate itself, to some extent, from plutocratic influence—turns out to avoid the evil of favoritism only very imperfectly and to avoid the evil of dogmatism not at all. Another way to contain or moderate the twin evils—by deepening democracy and enlarging the repertory of ways in which government and private enterprise can interact—is barely explored territory.

It may seem at first that the consequence of this line of reasoning is to suggest that because the means for defeating the twin evils are not readily at hand, except in a form that renders such means both limited and suspect, there will never be a good case for imposing restraints on free trade. The chastened votaries of strategic trade theory would have been right when they retreated from the implications of their own ideas, intimidated by the force of the twin evils argument.

Such a conclusion, however, would mistake the relation between economic and political possibility and would therefore miss what is most significant, both theoretically and practically, about the thesis we here examine. No country changes its political institutions or its way of making and implementing policy out of a philosophical attachment to a different form of political life. It changes them when it is persuaded that it must change them, when it comes to see them as a straitjacket that prevents it from moving and even from living.

However revolutionary it may be in its final outcome, such change is almost always undertaken in stumbling, uncertain steps, with the bric-a-brac of the conceptual and institutional materials available and the inconclusiveness that is characteristic of real action in the real world. We make up the means as we go along. As we make them up, we come to see in a new light and with different eyes the ends for the sake of which we forged them. Dissatisfaction with the established and available ways of doing what we believe we need to do is no reason not to do it; it is merely a reason to find better ways.

The case for the reconstruction of our political life is made from a hundred different inspirations, aroused in divergent areas of concern. One of them is the incitement of our desire to reconcile the engagement of a nation in the world economy with its ability to act on a vision of its own future and to preserve a sense of its own self.

The inference to draw from this discussion is therefore not that the restraints on trade that seem best in principle will never be best in practice. It is rather that the problem of free trade can be rightly understood and solved only as part of a much broader attempt to reimagine and to reinvent the forms of political and economic life. The case for the imposition of selective restraints on trade, at least in the situation of relative advantage, need not await the success of such an attempt at reimagination and reinvention. It need not await it because it forms part of it.

The Thesis of Self-Revision

A regime of international trade must be judged by the opportunities it creates for the experimental self-transformation of its participants as well as by its effective level of openness to trade flows. Free trade may be free in either or both these senses.

The gains of trade among countries vary directly with the range of opportunities offered by the trading regime for innovation in the practices and institutions of the trading partners. These benefits cannot adequately be construed simply on the basis of established or constructed comparative advantage in the international division of labor. They vary as well according to the degree of effective freedom that the trading nations enjoy to innovate in the ways in which they organize their productive and commercial practices as well as their governmental and economic institutions. A worldwide regime of free trade may either strengthen or weaken this freedom of experimental innovation. The incorporation into our thinking about free trade of this second level of concern requires a change in some of our theoretical assumptions. It also suggests a direction for the development of an international trade regime diverging from the direction that has prevailed in recent history.

This third proposition is the most general in scope and the most far-reaching in implication of these three theses. Its scope is not simply free trade understood as open commerce in goods and services among independent countries. It applies in the most general sense to our thinking about market activity, conducted, as market activity must normally be, against the background of a division of labor. It hardly matters, from the standpoint of the ideas that are central to this thesis, whether the market and the division of labor have as their setting the whole world or some tiny fraction of humanity. The thesis applies to free trade; worldwide free trade is, if only in its scope, the limiting case of a market-oriented division of labor.

The thesis addresses the relation between the moves we make within a framework of trade and the evolution of the framework. In thinking about the advantages and disadvantages of free trade, it is misleading to focus solely on the degrees and forms of restraints on trade. We need to consider as well the extent to which the rules of the trading regime encourage or inhibit the self-transformation of the trading partners. If free trade is achieved at the cost of heavy inhibitions on such self-transformation, it is likely to be bought at too high a price. If it advances in a way avoiding such inhibitions and encouraging self-revision, its benefits will be enhanced.

A crucial premise of the thesis of self-revision is that just as there exist alternative ways to realize the abstract conception of a market economy in a set of detailed practices and institutions, so there are also, at a second order, alternative ways to realize, in detailed practices and institutions, the regime of free trade among market economies. A major virtue of such a regime will be to permit, and even to encourage, participating countries that are parties to the regime to diverge experimentally in the type of market economy they establish.

The intuitive kernel of the thesis of self-revision lies therefore in a contrast between two hypothetical directions for the advancement of a trading regime. Under the first direction, the further the regime advances, the less room there is for the participants to diverge in their institutions and practices, at least in those defining the organization of the market economy. The rules of the trading regime will gradually incorporate ever more stringent requirements for the way each of those parties is organized: for example, assumptions about the content and scope of the rights of private property and limits on the ways government and private firms can work together, even when the public-private collaboration has only an indirect effect on trade. The development of the trading regime will therefore be associated with institutional convergence among the trading parties: the more fully realized the ideal of free trade, the greater the level of institutional convergence. The trading regime will be a straitjacket—according to its supporters, a golden straitjacket, necessary and even providential—but a straitjacket nevertheless.

Under the second direction, the advancement of free trade will not mean more institutional convergence imposed by the rules of the trading regime. There may be swings between periods of convergence and periods of divergence, but they will be not be driven by the rules and requirements of free trade. The point of the regime of free trade will not be to organize trade among entities that specialize in the production of different goods and services but that increasingly organize their economies in the same way, the better to produce those different things. The point will be to advance openness to foreign trade in the presence of difference: difference in the organization of the economy and the society as well as in the content of what is produced.

Those who take this second direction will refuse to regard the maximization of free trade as the commanding principle of the trading regime. Instead, if they are attached to free trade by the recognition of its practical advantages in the particular circumstances in which these advantages are most significant, they will want to reconcile divergence of institutions with openness to trade. Such a reconciliation, rather than the maximization of free trade, will, in their minds, count as the preeminent goal of the trading regime. No one will then suppose it either a necessity or a virtue to wear the straitjacket advocated by the defenders of the first direction.

The thesis of self-revision claims that the second direction is to be preferred decisively to the first. This claim may seem uncontroversial. In fact, it contradicts some of the assumptions that continue to shape the debate about free trade and protection. Its practical implications conflict with the way in which the regime of free trade has in fact developed.

There are two reasons to expect that the second direction for understanding and advancing free trade will prove superior to the first. One of these reasons is specific to the strategic requirements for the promotion of free trade; the other reason transcends the debate about free trade altogether and touches on our assumptions about the nature and conditions of economic growth.

The specific and strategic reason is that the acceptance of the straitjacket view puts the cause of free trade at odds with all the interests and values that donning the straitjacket of institutional convergence inevitably excludes. Free trade under that dispensation imposes a powerful constraint on the development of the institutional arrangements in which distinctions of culture and vision must be embodied. Without such institutional embodiment those differences risk becoming mere folklore, floating, as cultural idiosyncrasies, over the outcome of worldwide institutional convergence.

Moreover, each country would find in its adherence to the program of global free trade an obstacle to its ability to experiment with the policies, practices, and institutions useful to the goal that, for now and for an indefinite time in the future, enjoy the greatest appeal throughout the world: to organize a form of economic growth and of technological and organizational innovation that is socially inclusive and subversive of extreme and rigid divisions between the advanced and the backward sectors of each national economy.

The other, more basic and general basis for the superiority of the second direction over the first has to do with the character of growth and innovation and with their relation to free trade. One of the assumptions of the argument for the first direction is the idea that a market economy has a single, natural or necessary content, manifest in its legal institutions of property, contract, and corporate enterprise and in the legal provisions by which it ensures that the market-based allocation of resources will not ordinarily be overturned by either government or society. This assumption supports a defective picture of the freedom the market economy requires: a freedom to combine factors of production within an institutional framework of market activity that can be taken for granted. According to this picture, the framework can be left unchallenged and unchanged so long as it suffers from no instance of "market failure": any inequality in power or in information that undermines competition and distorts the signaling role of prices.

This view of the type of freedom central to a market economy depends for its authority on the prejudice of institutional fetishism with respect to the market: the false idea that the market has a natural form, or at least a form the superiority of which has been determined through a long evolutionary winnowing out. Once we rid ourselves of this assumption, we can radicalize the idea of economic freedom. What we should want is not simply freedom to combine factors of production within an institutional setting that we remain incapable of challenging and powerless to change;

it is freedom as well to renovate the institutional ideas and arrangements that define this setting. Anything less represents the sacrifice of an opportunity to a superstition.

The significance of this opportunity becomes clear when we consider its place in an account of the social requirements of economic growth. Here are the rudiments of a view of that place.

In the short term, economic growth depends on the relation between the costs of producing goods and services, as measured in the unit of exchange and as reflected in the real rate of interest, considered in relation to the opportunities for gain through production and exchange. In this short term, economic growth varies chiefly with the productivity of labor.

In the long term, economic growth requires the application of our causal knowledge of the world to the tasks of production. In this long term, what matters most is our success in producing machines that can do for us, according to formula, whatever we have learned how to repeat so that we can turn our energy and attention increasingly to the not yet repeatable.

In the protracted middle term, however, economic growth requires, above all, cooperation: it is a social process disguised as an economic one. Innovation is as indispensable as cooperation. Innovation presupposes cooperation, whether it is innovation in technologies, practices, organizations, or ideas. Cooperation withers without innovation. Nevertheless, innovation and cooperation are also at odds: every innovation threatens to break apart some piece of the set of claims and expectations that each collective participant—each segment of the labor force—has with regard to the other participants. The established regime of cooperation is embedded in this carapace of rights and expectations. Any threat to the carapace will be received as a threat to the regime.

A powerful incitement to hasten the tempo and to extend the scope of economic growth results when we succeed in establishing practices and arrangements of cooperation, in the firm or in the economy and society at large, that moderate the tension between the twin imperatives of cooperation and innovation. The proper goal of this effort is the development of an innovation-friendly practice of cooperation—the more hospitable to innovation, the better.

We never have a self-evident route to this advance. The advance can occur only through laborious and contested experiments with the arrangements for cooperation and with the institutions for production and exchange. It requires repeated and sustained fiddling with the institutional forms of the market economy.

Any approach to the understanding and development of free trade that inhibits or truncates such experimentation will impose an unacceptable cost on our practical interests, including our stake in growth and innovation. It will open up a wound, as onerous as it is unnecessary, within our practical interests. The very real but conditional gains of trade on the basis of established or achieved comparative advantage will be set in conflict with our larger stake in growth and innovation.

The best way to grasp the significance of the thesis of self-revision is to explore its implications for the reform of the world trading system. In fact, this thesis is incompatible with at least the first two of the four organizing principles on which the present system rests, and possibly with all four. The four principles are the choice of the maximization of free trade as the commanding goal of the trading regime; the incorporation into the program of free trade of the commitment to a particular type of market economy—the type now established in the North Atlantic countries—mistakenly understood as the natural and necessary form of such an economic order; the understanding of an open world economy as one in which goods and services (and, in an expanded view, capital as well) are free to cross national frontiers but people are not; and the willingness to accept wage labor as the preponderant form of free work in that economy, no matter how much tainted by a degree of economic duress that turns the contract between employer and employee into a sham.

To recognize the implications of the thesis of self-revision is to understand why it makes no sense, even from the standpoint of an interest in the creation of an open world economy, to take the maximization of free trade as the commanding principle of the global trading system. To elevate free trade to the status of an end in itself, pursued without regard to the power of experimental self-revision the trading partners may enjoy, is not to serve free trade; it is to undermine it. Free trade will flourish when the rules of the world trading system are designed to reconcile openness and diversity, not to suppress diversity in the name of openness.

Stated abstractly, this principle may seem unexceptionable. However, to imagine what its realization requires in the circumstances of the contemporary world is to show how it becomes controversial in practice. Consider the extreme instance at the present time of the destruction of the power of self-revision: the functional equivalent to the nineteenth-century gold standard, widely adopted by many Latin American countries in the closing decades of the twentieth century. In its heyday the gold standard, instituted to govern the commercial and monetary relations among the richest countries of that time, had the intended effect of making the level of economic activity depend on the level of business confidence. Tying the hands of government was not, for the architects of that monetary regime, its cost; it was its point.

Today there is a functional equivalent to the gold standard. However, the developing countries rather than the richest economies provide its chief field of application. A particular combination of policies defines the content of this equivalent: acceptance of a low level of domestic saving; consequent dependence on foreign saving to finance national development; openness of the capital account to facilitate the flow of capital in and out of the national economy; priority accorded to the interests of domestic and foreign rentiers over workers and producers; and insistence on a version of fiscal responsibility emphasizing restraint on public spending rather than enhancement of the tax take. This combination represents a functional equivalent to the gold standard because, like that standard, it treats the dependence of national governments on financial confidence as a solution rather than as a problem, an automatic antidote to populist and nationalist adventurism in the management of an economy.

It is not enough for a developing country to reject the functional equivalent to the gold standard; it is necessary for it to take measures that safeguard its ability to pursue a heretical strategy of development. In particular, it needs to raise a shield over initiatives subordinating the requirements of financial confidence—the religion of the capital markets as they are now organized—to the interests of the real economy. The generic requirement for success in the raising of a shield over national heresy is the mobilization of national resources—physical, financial, and human: up to the limit of a war economy without a war.

Consider the most constant components of this shield. The shield over heresy requires a forced high level of domestic saving—achieved through tightening of the links between saving and production both within and outside the existing capital markets and through the development of new ways of mobilizing saving for production—for example, the channeling of some mandatory pension saving into governmentally established but independently, professionally, and competitively managed venture capital funds. It presupposes the rejection of any management of the public debt resulting in a real rate of interest that spells the euthanasia of producers and the sacrifice of their interests to the interests of rentiers. It may demand an effort to keep high reserves (while mitigating the cost of maintaining them), achieved by a form of export-oriented growth that is the counterpart to import substitution and to the deepening of the domestic market rather than an alternative to such substitution and deepening. It counsels the safeguarding of these reserves by strong temporary controls on capital flows, without any bias against a fully convertible currency as an ultimate goal. It needs the pursuit of a policy of fiscal realism and fiscal sacrifice, even at the cost of the ability to conduct fiscal policy countercyclically, not to please the financial markets but, on the contrary, to make governments less dependent on their approval. It implies a willingness to rely, for the extraction of a high tax take, on whatever tax will allow for the highest take with the least disruption to established incentives to work, save, and invest, in particular the most neutral of all taxes, the comprehensive, flat-rate value-added tax. There must be such a willingness even at the cost of injustice in the design of the take tax; what is lost, by way of progressive, redistributive effect on the revenue-raising side of the budget, may be gained in double on its spending side. Above all, such relatively minor effects of compensatory redistribution through tax-and-transfer must be sustained and magnified by a more fundamental broadening of economic and educational opportunity.

The combined and cumulative effect of these different elements in the shield over heresy is to prevent governments from having to kneel down before the domestic and international financial markets. It is to widen their room for maneuver—the very room that both the classical gold standard and its latter-day functional equivalent so strikingly narrowed. It is to achieve some of the effect of wartime resource mobilization without having to fight.

The first two elements in this shield over heresy demand comment. It is a truth well established that "saving transitions"—major increases in the level of national saving—are more the consequence than the cause of economic growth. This theoretical proposition, however, fails to take account of the strategic value of high levels of forced saving and accumulated reserves (by countries that remain only imperfectly able to borrow in the currency) as a guarantee of independence in the early stages of a heretical development strategy.

A forced heightening of the level of domestic saving will, however, prove futile or pernicious if unaccompanied by arrangements ensuring that saving is channeled into production rather than dissipated in a financial casino. A paradoxical legacy of the Keynesian intellectual innovations of the mid-twentieth century in economic thinking is to deny us the ideas and even the words with which to formulate the problem of the relation between saving and production or productive investment. Under accounting categories that make aggregate saving necessarily equivalent to aggregate investment, we cannot even pose the problem.

Under the influence of a practice of economic analysis that treats the established market in capital as the incarnation of market rationality, except insofar as it is tainted by demonstrable and localized forms of "market failure," we have no reason to treat the relation of saving to production as a problem. Here we have an example of the power of institutional fetishism—the identification of the abstract conception of a market economy with a particular, historically contingent set of market arrangements. This fetishism continues to exercise a far-reaching and unrecognized influence over our economic ideas, within the debate about free trade and far beyond it.

The truth, however, is that institutions of production, exchange, and finance may be designed in ways that either tighten or loosen the links between saving and production. The extent to which the saving of society becomes available to production or productive investment is no mere matter of words. It cannot be deduced from abstractions or discovered by pure analysis. It is an empirical fact, varying in accordance with the arrangements by which we channel, or fail to channel, saving into production.

There are significant differences among contemporary advanced economies in the extent to which their economic institutions do this work. Nevertheless, in all of them by far the major part of the financing of production results from the retained earnings of firms. In all of them the vast pools of saving held in banks and in stockmarket portfolios have only an episodic or oblique connection to what is in theory the central role of the capital markets: to finance the productive activity of society. To tighten the link between saving and production through institutional innovations in the way of connecting them is not only possible, it is also necessary if an economic shield is indeed to be raised over economic heresy.

The functional equivalent to the gold standard is simply the extreme instance of a distinctive attitude to national development and to the construction of an open world economy. It is an attitude preaching obedience instead of defiance, institutional convergence instead of institutional diversity, and the acceptance of established comparative advantages instead of the invention of new ones. This attitude should be replaced, according to the thesis of self-revision, by an outlook that asks of each rule proposed for the governance of world trade both what it contributes to the opening of the world economy and how it reinforces the power of self-revision enjoyed by each trading country. The goal is to ensure the maximum of openness to the outside world that is consistent with the maximum capacity for self-revision at home.

The only credible restraints on internal organization that can be imposed in the name of an open world economy concern the capacity for resistance and dissent by strong, independent individuals and associations. Without such a capacity, society loses its power to create alternative visions of its own future and to act on them: the prohibition of slavery and child labor, the right to organize political parties, trade unions, and other associations; the right to challenge established power and to propagate subversive ideas. The forms of self-revision deserving of special support are those that enable countries to reinvent their comparative advantages and to shift labor from repeatable activities, undertaken by machines, to those activities that we do not yet know how to repeat.

For similar reasons, the thesis of self-revision conflicts with the second organizing principle of the established approach to global free trade, the incorporation of a particular version of the market economy into the rules of the world trading system. Once relieved of the burden of institutional superstition, universal free trade does indeed presuppose the worldwide diffusion of market economies. The market-oriented division of labor will be stronger in intensity and broader in scope if it goes all the way down, from the organization of the global economy to the dealings among economic agents in each of the countries that participate in the world trading system. However, if the arguments offered in support of the thesis of self-revision are right, vigorous national experimentation with the alternative institutional forms of the market is desirable even from the narrow standpoint of the enhancement of free trade.

Two of the implications of this principle deserve emphasis because of their practical significance for the organization of world trade. We should resist an expansion of property rights that, under the label of intellectual property, turns all innovations into proprietary assets. Moreover, we should refuse to prohibit as "subsidies" the market-trumping initiatives by which governments and societies create new kinds of markets, opening access to more resources for more people in more ways. A subsidy should be sanctioned only when its distorting effect on trade is direct and unequivocal. Even then, a country should be allowed to insist on the distortion and allowed to compensate its trading partners for the right to practice the proscribed subsidy if it serves aims that are more than merely economic (for example, the subsidization of a sector of the economy as support for a way of life that is valued as part of the national experience).

The thesis of self-revision fails to contradict with the same clarity the third organizing principle of the present regime of global trade: the stark contrast between its treatment of the movement of goods and services (to which many wish to add, by analogical extension, the movement of capital) and its treatment of the movement of people. Yet in many subtle ways this contrast is incompatible with the ideas and the interests underlying that thesis.

Free trade in goods and services is not unconditionally beneficial; its value depends on the conditions specified by the three theses presented here. Free movement of labor across national frontiers is unfeasible as an immediate goal. Its extension arouses a multitude of practical problems (the rights and interests of labor and the financing of social entitlements in the receiving countries, the loss of human capital in the receiving countries) that demand difficult solutions. The generic form of these solutions is to dispense the remedy in increasing doses: the expansion of the right to movement in small, cumulative steps; the layered grant of entitlements to foreign workers, from temporary work permits to full citizenship; and the development of arrangements to compensate countries for the formation of the skilled workers they lose to other countries.

In addition to the formidable practical obstacles it would need to overcome, the expansion of a right to cross national frontiers calls for a revolution in the understanding of nationality. It requires that we come to see the role of national difference in a world of democracies as a form of moral specialization within humanity. The basis for the appeal and authority of this specialization is the belief that humanity can develop its powers most fully only by developing different forms of life, housed in different institutional orders. This translation of moral difference into institutional divergence would pose a threat to the freedom of the individual if he were not free to escape the social world into which he happens to have been born and join another one.

In the absence of adequate dosage, preparation, and compensation, the extension of the right to cross national frontiers will prove self-defeating. It will dissolve, together with the sense of engagement in a shared national community, support for the sacrifices needed to sustain a high level of social entitlements. It may also help create a political reaction that ensures its own undoing.

Nevertheless, despite all the practical and moral difficulties with which it must contend, the step-by-step extension of the right of labor to cross national frontiers has a close relation to the values and interests supporting an open world economy. It represents by far the most effective instrument for the attenuation of extreme inequalities among nations and for the quickening of the pace of experimentation with the arrangements, methods, and products of economic activity.

That the peoples of the world should be in direct communion, their ideas and experiences jumbled by a trading of place as well as of products, that there should an endless flow of strangers in the midst of every nation, that the walls separating humanity should be thus torn down in the realities of direct encounter among individuals—all this represents the most radical realization of the idea of an open world economy and the most powerful inducement to collective self-transformation.

This thesis of self-revision is at once the most general of these three theses about free trade and the one that has the most direct significance for the criticism and reform of the system of world trade. What is its relation to the other two theses?

The circumstance in which one economy comes within striking distance of another is, according to the thesis of relative advantage, the situation in which the case for imposing restraints on free trade is likely to be strongest. However, the case will not be made unless, when it imposes restraints on trade in such a situation, a government avoids committing the twin evils of favoritism and dogmatism. To enjoy the power to impose the restraints without succumbing to the evils, a country must trust to the deepening of democracy rather than to the hardening of bureaucracy—the thesis of politics over economics. A country's interest in not having to deal with the present form of globalization and of free trade on a passive, take-it-or-leave-it basis will provide further encouragement to the reconstruction of its political life and of its administrative practices.

The theoretical and practical approach to free trade suggested by the combination of the theses of relative advantage and of politics over economics turns out to be incomplete, both in theory and in practice. It is incomplete in theory because it is only a fragment of a more general way of thinking about the market-oriented division of labor, whether an international division of labor among economies governed by independent states or a domestic division of labor among producers within a single national economy. A defect of the established way of thinking is that it fails to acknowledge the extent to which the benefits of trade among specialized producers are relative.

Such benefits are relative to the consequences of the trading regime for the ability of the trading partners, whether national economies or particular firms, continuously to reorganize themselves. The greater the restraints the regime imposes on this power of experimental and circumstantial self-transformation, the more limited its advantages will be: they will come poisoned. This idea is the theoretical point of the thesis of self-revision. From the perspective of this thesis, the first two theses amount to corollaries of a more general account of the relation between the practices of trade and the arrangements and assumptions on the basis of which they take place.

The view suggested by the theses of relative advantage and of politics over economics is incomplete practically as well as conceptually. They suggest a reorientation of national policy. However, when we try to translate them into a basis for thinking about the organization of the global trade regime, they seem to lead us into confusion and contradiction. The situation of relative advantage will come and go in the relations among particular economies. Countries will succeed or fail at the reforms that diminish the tribute selective trade policy pays to the twin evils.

No matter how flexible a world trading regime may be, however, it must operate according to general rules and shared conceptions. This fact underlies the practical significance of the thesis of self-revision. Each state must acquire and safeguard the practical instruments for the secure practice of national heresy in the choice of its development strategy and of its institutional arrangements. Not only must it avoid the functional equivalent to the gold standard, it must also ensure a mobilization of national resources sufficient to raise a shield over heresy.

The thesis of self-revision suggests a basis on which to develop an open world economy, and a system of global trade as part of it, owing nothing to the illusions and the interests that the argument of this essay has been designed to combat. There is a way of reconciling selective—and temporary—restraints on trade, in the situation of relative advantage, with the development of an open world economy. There is a way for free trade to enhance rather than to undermine the imperative of self-revision. No way, however, exists to achieve these ends without a redirection of the world trading system. I now map such a redirection.

Chapter 5

Proposals

● ○ ●

From an Analysis to a Program

The three theses about free trade proposed in the previous chapter have clear implications for the conduct of national policy. Their meaning for the organization of a world trading system, however, may seem far less evident. In fact, the first of the three, the thesis of relative advantage, may at first appear to be incompatible with any coherent trading regime designed on a worldwide scale. For it suggests that the case for moving toward free or freer trade may depend on the level of development of each trading partner in comparison to the level of the others. Relative backwardness can be determined only in particular relations among particular economies. By its very nature, relative backwardness constantly changes. For these reasons, the standard for allowing or disallowing freer trade that we can infer from the relative advantage thesis seems capable of realization only through an accumulation of bilateral arrangements. How could it ever inform a system of global trade?

The view of free trade for which I argue nevertheless has definite implications for the reform of the world trading system. It guides a criticism of the principles on which the present regime is based, and suggests a path for its reconstruction. The effort to work out these implications has theoretical as well as practical value: the programmatic consequences of the three theses shed further light on the way of thinking that they illustrate and justify.

Two precautions help clarify the character of the proposals advanced in the following pages.

The first precaution has to do with the nature of a programmatic argument. To be telling and useful, a program need not, indeed should not, be a blueprint. It should mark a direction and explore next steps to take, beginning from where we are here and now. Our understanding of transformative opportunity—of the adjacent possible—reveals the content of our insight into the actual.

A second precaution follows from this first as a corollary. In its particular content, a program like this one can have no lasting significance: it suggests how we can move in a certain direction, given the circumstance in which we find ourselves and the conceptual and institutional materials available to us. The sense of the direction lasts longer than the definition of the next steps. Nevertheless, as we take these steps, we must revise our understanding of the direction, making choices—of interests, of ideals, of forms of life and organization—that the steps themselves prompt or force us to make. What lasts longest of all—and has the most general intellectual significance—is the mode of thought developed through such a programmatic exercise. It is a mode of thought that seeks to loosen the shackles of rationalization: to show us how we can discount the necessity, the naturalness, and the authority of present arrangements without failing to recognize either the forces that shape them or the constraints that they impose.

The object to which this exercise is devoted has immense practical interest: the form and fate of globalization. The global trading regime is the heart of the emerging form of globalization. The larger idea animating this programmatic proposal for the organization of world trade is that we need not approach globalization on a take-it-or-leave-it basis, resigning ourselves to have only more of it or less of it, or to have it happen more quickly or more slowly. We can have it, more of it, on different terms. We can reimagine it and remake it.

The World Trade Regime and Its Reconstruction

The emerging world trading system rests on four principles. If the argument of this book is right, we should replace each of these four principles by a different organizing idea.

The first principle of the present system is to accept the maximization of free trade as the proper goal of the world trading regime. Free trade deserves no such role. It is a means, not an end. It is capable of producing very great benefits to the parties that engage in it. However, those benefits depend on certain empirical conditions, which may fail to be fulfilled. Moreover, their reality, even in the many circumstances in which they are there to be enjoyed, depend for their vitality and benignity on a broader context of chances for experimentation. An important species of such tinkering is experiment with the legal and institutional form of the market economy itself.

The argument for the advantages of free trade on the basis of international specialization represents a special case of the argument for a market economy of specialized producers within a division of labor. To produce and to retain its benefits, free trade must be implemented in a way remaining faithful to the attributes that can make the market economy so powerful an instrument for the creation of wealth: the ability of such an economy to make use of everyone's productive energy through decentralized, self-directed initiative; its implicit ideal of an organized anarchy dispensing with hierarchy and dogma as ways to organize coexistence; its openness to novelty so long as someone wants the novelty badly enough to be willing to sacrifice and to pay for it; and its power to turn back on its own practices and arrangements the experimental impulse it arouses.

To accept the maximization of free trade as the organizing principle of world trade is to substitute the narrow dogma for the broad project and to mistake a device for a goal. Sometimes the expansion of free trade will promote a pluralist experimentalism in economic life. At other times it will not. In certain forms and circumstances it will unleash the most promising productive forces, although it may also create losers, who may then deserve to be compensated, and require to be retrained. In other forms and circumstances it may simply condemn a national economy to remain trapped in a position of relative backwardness from which it cannot readily escape. One of the goals of this book has been to suggest categories and standards by which to distinguish among such situations.

The extent to which countries may benefit from the advantages of free trade without being harmed by its dangers is not fixed. It depends on exactly how the system of free trade is organized. By demoting free trade to the status of conditional means rather than unconditional end, we free ourselves to imagine and to develop arrangements that allow for more free trade with less suppression of institutional novelty and of potential for production.

The second principle on which the emerging form of globalization has been based is the practical identification of universal free trade with the enforced propagation of a particular form of the market economy. The method is the incorporation into the trade rules (or into the requirements of membership in the World Trade Organization) of constraints and commitments imposing adherence to a narrow institutional formula. The focus of these demands may be a certain approach to defining and protecting the content and the scope of property rights. Or it may be a particular attitude toward limits on governmental activism in economic life. An example of the former is an expansive understanding of rights in intellectual property. An example of the latter is an inclusive prohibition of "subsidies": all governmental allocations of resources overturning the market-shaped allocation, even if the intervention has no direct distorting effect on foreign trade and even if it forms part of an effort to create a new kind of market, to which new economic agents may have access in new ways.

The consequence is to entangle the cause of free trade, and more generally of globalization, in the campaign for worldwide institutional convergence. This entanglement arouses the adversaries of the latter to oppose the former. It weakens rather than strengthens the connection of free trade to the stake in decentralized initiative that is central to the attractions of the market.

A third principle of the emerging system of globalization and free trade is its willingness to analogize freedom for the movement of capital to freedom for the movement of goods and services and its unwillingness to apply any such analogy to the free flow of labor. It is only a slight exaggeration to say that a free global economy has been understood to be one in which things but not people are free to move. Many have wanted to bestow on capital, the most abstract thing, the same right enjoyed by things, under conventional free trade, to cross national frontiers.

Nothing in principle could be more fundamental to a project of globalization or to a doctrine of free trade than the extent of the freedom of movement each accords to things, capital, and people. A world in which freedom of movement is granted to one of the three but not to the others is radically different from one in which all three win freedom together. Both in turn differ greatly from a world in which capital wins, but people are denied, the freedom of movement accorded to things. There are, however, few topics in economic theory or in policy debate that have received less benefit of theoretical penetration. Here special pleading rules: a mish-mash of blanket ideological prejudice and of ad-hoc adjustment to unprincipled practical constraint.

It has often been argued that both goods and capital move so that people need not move. According to this idea, capital flows reinforce the effect of trade in goods: in addition to making all national trading partners (although not all particular firms) richer; they also begin to diminish inequality in the returns to labor. Just in case people should fail to acknowledge the bearing of this calculus on their actions, they are prohibited, by the conventional doctrine of economic freedom, from moving.

There is a straightforward practical objection to the line of reasoning that seeks to assimilate freedom for capital flows to freedom for trade in goods: relatively little capital moves. Moreover, the part that does move—particularly if it is in the form of short-term speculative finance—exercises a power of disturbance out of all proportion to its scale or to whatever contribution it may make to production. Even today, at the beginning of the twenty-first century, net capital flows, in relation to the GDP of major national economies, remain smaller than they were in the earlier, nineteenth-century episode of globalization. Empirical study has confirmed that the vast preponderance of funds available for investment remain at home, in the country of its origin, despite the increasing freedom of movement and legal security won by capital under the aegis of the present form of globalization.

Yet the remainder of capital that does move can readily make governments hostage to surges of panic or greed unless those governments have raised shields over heresy. Developing countries will have to mobilize their own resources rather than depend on foreign capital as fuel for their growth. They will need to stand ready to impose temporary and selective but forceful restraints on the movement of capital even when they want in the end complete convertibility of their currency.

Despite all these objections—of theory, prudence, and experience—to the association of the cause of free trade with the acceptance of free movement of capital, the rush to establish this association as a feature of the emerging form of globalization was halted only by two forces. The first was the international financial crisis of 1997–1999. The second was the resistance of the two most important developing economies: China and India.

The alacrity with which freedom for capital flows has been defended contrasts with almost universal adherence to the assumption that no such freedom should or can be granted to labor. Yet no thesis would seem to be more characteristic of conventional, market-oriented thinking, both within and outside economics, than the idea that labor should be free to work where it will find its best reward. Moreover, greater allowance for the mobility of labor dwarfs all other initiatives in its potential to diminish inequalities among countries. Enhancement of the right of labor to cross national frontiers is the practical point at which standard arguments of efficiency and equity most clearly and fully converge.

A fourth principle underlying the established project of free trade and globalization is the acceptance of wide disparities in the rewards and rights of labor, among countries as well as within them. That labor may be better rewarded in some societies than in others has always been an assumption of thinking about trade conducted on the basis of comparative advantage. The simplest and most persistent model of trade has been trade between a capital-rich North, in which labor is more productive and better paid, and a labor-rich South, in which labor is less productive and worse paid. Were the freedom to trade on this basis to be compromised, trade might seem to lose much of its point.

An unqualified right to reward labor unequally is ordinarily distinguished from the much more controversial issue of labor standards: the framework of rights within which labor will be exchanged for a wage. The representatives of organized labor in the North clamor for limits on the extent to which labor can be deprived of rights in the trading countries of the South. They demand that minimal standards for the protection of the labor and for the elimination of the worst abuses be imposed as a condition of accession to the global trading system and that these standards be incorporated into bilateral and regional trade agreements. Although some in both North and South resist this demand as an excuse for protectionism and criticize it as harmful to those whom it would benefit, a growing body of opinion defends the linkage of free trade to labor standards. This body of opinion finds allies in those who seek an analogous linkage to environmental standards.

Thus, the acceptance of stark inequalities in the rewards and status of labor as an indispensable predicate of a trading regime has come increasingly to be qualified. Wage inequalities among as well as within countries are to be allowed, no matter how extreme. Even within this established practice, however, the treatment of labor must pass a certain minimum threshold of legal protection. Wage labor must not cease to be free labor. The form of a free contract between employer and employee must have some practical reality.

In this qualified form, the fourth principle on which the emerging world trade regime has come to rely can be summarized in a single idea, rarely made explicit: labor can and even should be unequally rewarded, according to its abundance relative to capital and therefore as well according to its productivity. Nevertheless, there should be a point at which this inequality stops. That point is the circumstance in which wage labor represents a continuation of slavery under the disguise of free contract. In such a circumstance, the employment contract conceals a measure of dependence and oppression so extreme as to make a mockery of the contractual form in which the employment relation is couched.

To make explicit this assumption is to disclose a source of perplexity and trouble to which both our received beliefs and our established arrangements fail to do justice. The surface expression of the problem is that the distinction between the wage return to labor and the legal status of labor is no more than a matter of degree. The legal privileges enjoyed, and the legal disabilities suffered, by the laborer are worth money. They help set the terms on which the capitalist and the worker will strike the wage deal, and they may have a quantifiable economic expression for the latter as well as for the former.

Moreover, the wage may be so low, and so incapable of ensuring the worker of the necessities of life and the material requirements of personal dignity, that the labor standards guaranteed to him may prove to be an empty promise. Indeed, the same circumstances of relative abundance of labor that help explain the low wage may also weaken the ability of the workers, even when organized, to use legal rights to obtain economic advantage. The point is not that legal rights are powerless to transform the relation between capital and labor. It is that minimalist labor standards, such as those that are the object of the present compromise, may not be enough.

However, as soon as we consider the need to make these standards more stringent, we come up against the deeper side of the problem: the nature and position of economically dependent wage labor as a premise of the market economy and of its international form in a regime of universal free trade. Free labor has been defined historically, by contrast to slavery and serfdom. It assumes three principal forms: self-employment, association or partnership, and wage labor. Self-employment and association are so closely connected in practice as well as in conception that they can barely be distinguished; partnership, broadly understood, is simply self-employment in cooperation. Wage labor has been by far the most important of the three forms: important in the numbers of people to which it applies and important in its influence in shaping our assumptions and arrangements for organizing the division of labor under a market economy.

But can and does economically dependent wage labor in fact resemble the slavery to which it is supposed to be the alternative? This question, so strange to us that we have trouble taking it seriously, was central to the institutional and ideological controversies of the nineteenth century as well as to the debates in political economy that gave birth to the teaching of free trade and to the doctrine of comparative advantage. The words and the settings of those quarrels are too distant to be recovered. However, the issue they addressed did not vanish when they lost their force. On the contrary, it has now become urgent and worldwide. We must struggle with it in a different situation and with different words.

The contractual form of wage labor may accommodate and conceal radically different realities. It may serve to transmit privilege. In some of the rich North Atlantic economies of the early twenty-first century, especially the American economy, wage inequality became the fastest growing type of inequality: many of the most advantaged members of society received their income in the form of salaries or of quasi-wage benefits.

In other parts of those same North Atlantic countries, at the same historical moment, as well as in the most advanced sectors of the major developing economies, union organization and direct legal regulation of the employment relation had worked together to improve the condition of labor. It had often improved it, however, to the benefit of a class of relatively privileged insiders and at the cost of the unorganized and unprotected outsiders. The decline of mass-production industry—the old historical base of trade-unionism, the emergence, with worldwide trade, of a global labor pool including hundreds of millions of Chinese and Indian workers, and the failure to establish the institutions that would expand access to the market economy and to advanced practices of production and learning—all these factors converged to generalize the experience of insecurity and weaken the value of the old arrangements designed to guarantee that wage labor would be free labor.

And in yet other parts of the world or in poorer sectors of the economies of the richest countries, wage labor remained subject to dependence and insecurity so extreme, and the wage level remained so little above the return needed to keep the worker alive and working, that the reality of the employment relation belied its contractual form.

The ideal of a market economy can be most directly satisfied by free labor achieved through partnership or association when not through individual self-employment. It is only under such a regime that the idea of freedom to transact, to exchange, to cooperate, and to experiment can be realized most fully and universally. That wage labor should be the main form of free labor and that the most common condition of wage labor should be a degree of economic duress giving the lie to the contractual form of the employment relation are facts eroding the reality of the market ideal. A vast range of only partly understood consequences, economic as well as social and political, result from this erosion.

The worldwide project of the market economy, further confirmed and advanced through free trade, continues to rely on ways of organizing cooperation that are tainted by the coercive realities of economically dependent wage labor. This reliance is supposedly justified by unyielding practical constraints as well as by the unavoidable implications of a regime of private property for the relation between capital and labor. To reach a conclusion about whether the market economy and the world trading system should continue to rely, without complaint or qualification, on the preponderance of economically dependent wage labor, it is necessary to understand whether these justifications are well founded. They are not. The truth they contain is so incomplete as to mislead in the most important respects.

One class of justifications for the necessity of wage labor, dependent on the job and deprived of any significant share of ownership in the means of production, is purely practical: the buying of labor by those who represent the powers of accumulated capital would be the indispensable means to ensure both scale in production and discipline at work. By separating the decision to invest from the decision to work, it becomes possible to establish the large pool of assets needed to fund large enterprise. Moreover, the buying of the labor time of the worker dispossessed of enough property to work usefully and profitably for himself establishes a contractual basis for a discretionary power, the exercise of which cannot or should not be made fully contractual. The residue of discretionary authority, validated by law and contract but not devoured or paralyzed by them, becomes the means to direct, according to practical constraint and opportunity, the combination of people and machines.

This justification relies for its force on an assumption it fails to make explicit: no set of institutional arrangements for the organization of a market economy would fulfill these requirements without appealing to property-less wage labor as its characteristic way of marshalling cooperative effort. The argument from scale and discretion needs to be reinforced by an argument from property. A regime of private property, more or less like the one that has come to prevail in the course of modern Western history, is claimed to be necessary to the operation of a market economy.

Such a regime, according to this argument, requires that the owner have almost unconditional power over the resources at his command so long as he remains within the sharply defined boundaries of his property right. It also presupposes that the right extend freely in time, through an unbroken sequence of legitimate transactions and, ultimately, through the hereditary transmission of property. The mechanisms and standards of redistribution must not be so far-reaching that they eviscerate the combined workings of contract and property.

The strong form of this argument, in which few are able to believe today, is that a property regime designed on this model is intrinsic to the nature of a free economic and political order. The weak form of this argument, with far greater but unacknowledged authority, concedes that such a regime may not belong to the essential nature of such an order, if only because, being historical constructs, institutional arrangements lack essential natures. It nevertheless insists that any attempt to suppress and replace the present regime of private property by another way of organizing people's claims on one another will undermine economic and political freedom, destroying the basis of a market economy in the independent initiative of countless economic agents.

In either its strong or its weak form, this argument from property leads to the conclusion that in a market economy, based as a market economy supposedly must be on the familiar form of private property, claims to the control of the productive assets of society will end up very unequally distributed. Most people will need to sell their labor. The social rights and the private savings that may attenuate this need will in any event be insufficient to finance all but small businesses. Thus, the predominance of economically dependent wage labor in the organization of cooperative activity under a market economy emerges as the consequence of a combination of the argument from the imperatives of scale and discretion with the argument from the implications of private property.

The combination of the argument from scale and efficiency with the weak form of the argument from property depends for its force on the absence of alternative ways of organizing a decentralized economy on a basis that might reduce and eventually overcome the central role of economically coerced wage labor in such an economy. That it is at least possible to conceive of a market economy without such heavy reliance on wage labor (whether or not such labor is sold and performed under economic duress) can be inferred readily from a simple exercise in analysis.

The conventional idea of a market economy mixes together two notions that are not conceptually identical and that may not need to be practically joined. One notion is that of large numbers of economic agents, able to act on their own initiative and for their own account. This formulation emphasizes the multiplicity of independent economic agents. The other notion is that of the absoluteness of the power—absolute in scope and in time—that the owner enjoys over the resources under his command.

Not only are the two sides of this idea not necessarily conjoined, they may be inversely related in social and economic fact. The unified property right in its modern form is a relatively recent construction: the several powers it unites were in many periods of the history of law, the West as well as outside it, decomposed and vested in different types of rightholders. Under a decomposed property right regime, such rightholders then held simultaneously claims to different aspects of the same productive assets. (Feudalism represents an extreme instance of such a possibility.)

By decomposing the unified property right and vesting its component powers in different tiers of rightholders, we might create forms of decentralized claims on productive resources. Such claims might limit, as many past and present forms of property have, the absoluteness and the eternity of the right. At the same time, they might increase the number of agents with access to the underlying resources as well as the variety of terms on which the independent economic agents could make use of the resources. If we succeeded, we would have enhanced the first side of the conventional idea of property at the cost of the second. The traditional property right might survive. However, it would survive as only one regime among many, suitable to those forms of economic activity in which there is most reason to facilitate and to reward initiative undertaken at the risk of the entrepreneur and in the teeth of collective disbelief.

A consequence of such a change—indeed, one of its overriding goals—might be to make more productive resources and opportunities available to more people in more ways. A further outcome might be to deal with the imperatives of scale and discretion in productive activity in ways that over time would be less likely to organize production on the basis of a contrast between representatives of capital and sellers of labor.

We might do all this in theory, but would we and could we do it in fact? All depends on our success in creating alternative regimes of private and social property from the conceptual and institutional materials at hand. Our experiment might well eventually include allowing different regimes of private or social property to coexist experimentally within the same, now diversified market economy.

It is not the task of this work to explore the substance of such alternative property regimes or the ways in which they could emerge out of the present and historical systems of ownership.* However, it is a recurrent theme of this book that the same grounds we have for embracing a market economy and for building an open world

---

*For a discussion of such alternatives, see *False Necessity: Antinecessitarian Social Theory in the Service of Radical Democracy* Verso, 2001, pp. 195–206, 480–539, and *Democracy Realized: the Progressive Alternative,* Verso, 1998, pp. 133–212.

economy are also reasons to experiment, in each country and throughout the world, with the institutional forms of the market and of free trade.

The implications of this speculative argument about alternative property regimes for the status of labor now become clear. The greatest benefits of market exchange and free trade are placed in jeopardy to the extent that the wage labor on which the market and international trade systems now largely depend ceases to be free labor. An important attribute of a reformed world trading system is that it strengthen the impulses making free labor ever less like slavery.

In the light of these facts and arguments, we can rephrase the question about free wage labor and slavery and turn it into a series of connected questions to which a program for the reformation of the world trading system must give practical answers. What should be the common status of labor in a market-oriented division of labor, made universal by the world trading regime? How much different from slavery does wage labor (when rendered under economic duress) need to be for the idea of a free world economy of free workers to be realized in fact? What limitations on inequality in the wage return to labor among different societies are both feasible and necessary to ensure that the development of an open world economy takes place on the ground of really free labor? How is our conception of free trade in general and of comparative advantage in particular modified by the demand that it rest on a real, not just a sham, foundation of free labor?

The effort to link free trade to minimal labor standards, which represents the furthest horizon of the present compromise, is admittedly inadequate to the task presented by these connected questions. It may nevertheless represent a beginning if we reconsider and reanimate it in the light of these ideas.

Free Trade Reformed: The Reconciliation of Alternatives

This transformation in our way of thinking about free trade suggests the main lines along which the present world trading regime should be reformed. In considering these directives, it is important to bear in mind the qualifications mentioned at the outset: that, like any exercise in programmatic imagination, the following proposal should be understood as the marking of a direction and the choice of next steps; that any such direction can be explored at points relatively close to the present or relatively remote from it (I choose here an arbitrary point, neither very close nor very remote); and that, although the particulars of a program like this one are by nature circumstantial and ephemeral, the direction they exemplify may hold more lasting interest.

The elements of the proposal can be grouped under the heading of four counterprinciples that we should put in place of the four principles on the basis of which free trade is now being established throughout most of the world.

These considerations bring us to the counterprinciple that should occupy the place of the commitment to maximize free trade. It is to build, step by step, an open world economy in whatever way offers the best promise of reconciling global openness with room for national and regional diversity, deviation, heresy, experiment. The point is not to maximize free trade; it is to maximize the possibility of coexistence among different development strategies, institutional systems, and forms of social life, and then, on that basis, to advance freer trade. The result is not to insist on free trade in circumstances (such as the situation of relative advantage) in which free trade would discourage institutional divergence and heretical development.

Once this counterprinciple is established, it can develop in the direction of a qualified international pluralism. There must be limits to the national and regional experiments that the world trading system can accommodate if it is to remain faithful to the practical and moral interests animating it. Membership in the global trading order should not require adherence to any particular institutional version of the market economy or of political democracy. It may, however, proscribe extremes of disempowerment: the suppression within a country of opportunities for independent economic and political agency and consequently for challenge to the established way of doing things.

Such denials of opportunity for decentralized enterprise and contrarian action undermine the value of national and regional experiments for humanity, not just for citizens of the country in which such experiments take place. They limit the development of an open world economy by preventing firms, groups, and individuals within a country from taking the innovative initiatives that can fuel distinctive national strategies and specializations.

The formative goal of the trading regime should therefore be the reconciliation of alternative development strategies and alternative versions of economic, political and social pluralism rather than the maximization of free trade. A large part of the effort must be to moderate the tension between openness and diversity—diversity of both orientation and organization.

This commitment may at first seem to be almost entirely negative in its consequences. It is in fact rich in practical effects. The world should multiply, not restrict, opportunities for countries to opt out of the general trading regime. Such opt-out rights must be explicit, and they must be exercised through multilaterally agreed procedures. The exercise of the opt-out will face a natural constraint; a country will lose access to other countries' markets to the extent it closes its own market.

The expansion of the right to opt out of the universal trading regime, for a while and at a price, should be distinguished from any arbitrary historical exemption, such as the arrangements by which the rich countries of the late twentieth century succeeded in entrenching their agricultural protection when the World Trade Organization was first established. The prerogative to opt out should be ensured in the universal interest; it should not be reduced to the status of an odious privilege enjoyed by those who first sat at the banquet.

Such an approach is no novelty. It more closely resembles the arrangements existing under the General Agreement on Tariffs and Trade (GATT) than it does the subsequent WTO treaties. Yet it should not be understood as a retreat from the cause of an open world economy. Its effect is to prevent any fundamental opposition between our stake in diversity and our stake in openness. By the same token, its consequence is to keep the interest in openness from pushing the rules of world trade toward a lowest common denominator. The rules can then develop in detail, expressing a thick consensus, without suppressing national experiments, including the experiments in novel forms of economic, political, and social pluralism that they are unable to countenance.

The right to opt out has an importance within the way of thinking I here put forward that is brought into focus by the thesis of relative advantage: that the benefits of free trade are likely to be most limited and its dangers most pronounced among trading partners that are neither at comparable nor at very different levels of development; the relatively more backward economy lies within striking distance of the relatively more advanced one. Not only is it necessary for countries to be able to opt out of the general trading regime to be able to act in the light of this truth, it is also necessary for them to be able to do so in the form of specific bilateral arrangements rather than through a generalized secession from that regime. Any system sharply curtailing the right to opt out will make it impossible for countries to act on this proposition. As a result they will be condemned by the design constraints of the regime to suffer either more or less free trade than their position relative to their trading partners makes advisable.

To put the reconciliation of alternative pathways of development within an opening world economy in the place of the maximization of free trade as the commanding principle of world trade may seem to be a change of little or uncertain consequence. Its meaning will differ sharply, however, according to the assumptions we bring to it.

To the many who believe that there are no major alternatives and that all the countries of the world are inevitably converging on the same set of best practices and institutions, the substitution may appear to be a bothersome and misguided distraction. To them, its danger will lie chiefly in providing a pretext to restrict free trade and to slow down institutional convergence. To those others, however, who do believe that alternative pathways of development are both possible and necessary, the substitution will seem momentous. They will identify transformative opportunity where the votaries of convergence see only the marriage of costly illusion with shameless self-interest.

It forms no part of the intellectual program of this book to explore in detail the alternative trajectories of national development open to contemporary societies. That there are such alternatives, that the worldwide desire to reconcile economic growth with social inclusion depends on them, and that the future of the revolutionary belief in the ascent of ordinary men and women to greater life and power in turn depends on this reconciliation are all ideas central to my view. All along the way in the course of working out this argument I have suggested some of the basic building blocks and shared concerns of such alternatives and asked within what world economic order and under what trade regime they could flourish.

Consider two approaches. According to one position, attractively modest in its claims, the alternatives are local; it is the political-economic orthodoxy they resist that claims a universal authority. Why should the alternatives mirror this imperial ambition? Countries must find their way by combining elements of the falsely universal orthodoxy with innovations responsive to local constraint and opportunity.

The trouble is that only a universalizing heresy can effectively combat a universal orthodoxy. One of two situations will occur. If the deviation from the universal orthodoxy is undertaken for purely practical reasons, it is likely to be abandoned at the first sign of difficulty. The gravitational pull of the orthodoxy will prove irresistible. If the heresy is embraced on the basis of religious or cultural commitments transcending practical imperatives, it may counterbalance this pull, but only at the cost of losing contact with the experimentalist ideals that market economies and democratic polities have in common.

According to a second position, the heresies must themselves have shared features, shared enough to suggest for contemporary democratic societies and market economies a direction different from the one that now prevails. The local heresies must have these common attributes and offer the rudiments of a universalizing proposal if they are successfully to resist the universal orthodoxy.

Remember that the classical liberalism from which the doctrine of free trade arose was once itself a universalizing heresy: expressed and initiated in particular countries, yet conveying, from the outset, a message to all mankind.

It is, however, not only out of the requirements of successful opposition to the universal orthodoxy that the most successful and significant local heresies dare not and cannot be so local after all. It is also because all contemporary societies work with a relatively narrow and inelastic repertory of institutional arrangements and ideas. The institutional and ideological adventures of the twentieth century are finished; their conclusion has left contemporary societies in the grip of a small list of living options for the organization of different areas of social experience. This restrictive institutional canon is the fate of the present societies. To overthrow this fate it is necessary to enlarge that canon.

The struggle for such an enlargement is bound to take place under double sponsorship: the brutal rivalry of states, cultures, and classes and the potential appeal of the most powerful belief at work in the world—faith in the rise of ordinary men and women to a greater power and a higher life. This faith requires, if it is to advance, the radicalization of democracy, the economic and educational empowerment of the individual, and the construction of a form of economic growth and permanent innovation that is socially inclusive.

A fight to expand, under this aegis, the present repertory of forms of social, economic, and political organization must begin with the limited institutional arrangements and ideas at hand. Recombining and renovating these arrangements and ideas in the service of that creed or that rivalry, it can create greater difference, on the basis of democracy and experimentalism. It can do so, however, only by passing first through a narrow gateway.

This gateway is made up of the institutional and ideological innovations that would strengthen the collective power to create new and valuable difference in the world: difference in the institutional forms and the moral tenor of a free society. The identification of such innovations is the work of the universalizing heresy that would today oppose the universal political and economic orthodoxy.

A double paradox shapes this reality. Humanity can be become more unified only by seeking to develop in different directions. Nevertheless, it can develop more forcefully in different directions only by sharing in some elements of a common agenda of the deepening of democracy, the democratization of markets, and the economic and educational endowment of individuals.

This second position—of a universalizing heresy opposing the universal orthodoxy—rather than the first position—of a universal orthodoxy qualified by local heresies—motivates many of the arguments of this book. However, the replacement of the maximization of free trade by the reconciliation of alternative development trajectories as the organizing principle of international trade can find support and guidance in either position. Each of them gives it a different meaning. Both of them will oppose the skepticism of those who disbelieve in the existence of alternatives that are worth thinking about and fighting for.

Every powerful idea about society has some element of self-fulfilling prophecy. Every such prophecy struggles with the stubborn resistance of facts. To define the reconciliation of alternative pathways of national development within a world economy that becomes progressively more open as the commanding principle of the trading system is to establish a machine for the creation of collective difference. It is to support alternatives by making the world safer for them.

Free Trade Reformed: Experimenting with the Form of the Market Economy

The second counterprinciple to place at the foundation of world commerce is a resistance to any attempt to entangle the cause of free trade in the imposition of a particular species of market economy.

The trading rules must be so formulated as to presuppose and to foster alternative approaches to the understanding and the organization of the market economy. Once again, this counterprinciple may at first seem almost entirely negative. It nevertheless has affirmative implications. Consider them in two areas: the scope and content of property rights, particularly as applied to the treatment of intellectual property, and the definition and treatment of subsidies.

The rules of global free trade should minimize requirements of institutional conformity. They should hold open the possibility that the adherents to the conventional doctrine of free trade implicitly deny: that a market economy may assume institutional forms different from those that are now established—in the rich North Atlantic countries or anywhere else. The existing forms represent a subset of a larger, open-ended range of institutional possibilities or of directions for institutional innovation: innovation in the way of organizing a market economy itself.

This minimalism about markets creates space for the construction of comparative advantage by coordinated action between governments and firms. It also broadens the margin within which national governments can maneuver to create forms of the market economy that are more socially inclusive and more capable of providing economic opportunity in more ways to more people.

A lesson of historical experience is that it may be impossible radically to broaden access to the market economy, especially in the circumstances of very unequal societies, without changing the way in which that economy is organized. Once such national experimentation with the arrangements of the market economy gains strength, it may make possible an ideal that we have thus far nowhere seen realized: the experimental coexistence of different models of the market economy, including different regimes of private property and contract, within the same national economy.

The advance of universal free trade will no longer be predicated on a narrowing of local or national alternatives. It will not prevent the pursuit of a goal that holds great promise for humanity: the radicalization of our freedom to combine factors of production within an unchallenged framework of market institutions into a larger freedom to innovate continuously in the content of that framework and to do so, without crisis or confrontation, as part of the normal life of an economy.

This principled minimalism has a limit, the same limit underlying the idea that the goal of the world trading system should be to organize the coexistence of the divergent rather than to maximize the commerce of the convergent. The limit is the bias toward economic, social, and political pluralism, within countries as well as among them, that ought properly to be built into the rules of international trade. It should be built into those rules not only for the sake of the larger interests and values associated with such a pluralism but also for the sake of free trade itself and of its economic benefits: specialization with experimentalism is more promising, economically as well as socially and politically, than specialization without experimentalism. The requirements of experimentalism go all the way from the political and economic organization of the whole world to the internal organization of the firm, the workplace, and the school.

The rules of universal free trade must not entrench, as a requirement of accession to the regime that they establish, the acceptance of any particular system of contract and property rights. They should not operate on the mistaken supposition that such a system inheres in the nature of a market economy. Their legal and institutional spirit should be one of a liberating open-mindedness about the range of ways in which a market economy can be organized. Such an agnosticism would give practical effect to an underexploited teaching of the legal science of the period of 1850–1950: that there is no single natural and necessary legal and institutional form that a market economy need take, that diversity of such forms may require divergent regimes of property and contract, and that no market economy can be made significantly more inclusive without being reorganized.

One species of this minimalism about private rights has special importance, the species dealing with intellectual property (a subject to which the discussion of the fourth counterprinciple returns). A global trading regime hospitable to democratic experimentalism must not wed itself to the particular system of intellectual property that has come to be established in the rich North Atlantic countries and that, with considerable success, those countries have since attempted to impose on the whole of humanity. It is the peculiar character of that system of intellectual property to turn innovations into assets. The traditional arguments in favor of that approach resemble in structure the conventional case for the hereditary transmission of property: they combine an appeal to consequentialist arguments about incentives to innovate with the deployment of deontological arguments about the deserved rewards of invention. The frailties of each argument are remedied by resort to the other one, and the two together pretend to an authority that neither of them alone would be able to enjoy.*

The present arrangements for the protection of intellectual property are in no sense a natural and necessary implication of the commitment to establish a market economy. They are the contingent and extreme result of a particular way of encouraging innovators. They threaten to harm the very interests they are supposedly designed to safeguard.

There are alternatives. The least that can be demanded from the global trading regime with respect to intellectual property is that it not require those who join to forswear all such alternatives. For example, some countries could return to a road considered but not taken in nineteenth-century Europe: government-funded rewards for invention and public financing of research in exchange for the immediate placement of the financed and rewarded inventions in the common property of mankind. Nothing in the rules of global trade should prevent such an experiment.

Another aspect of the minimalism about market economies that the global trading regime should embrace is a decisive change in the treatment of so-called subsidies. Here the focus is not on the divergent paths by which a market economy may shape, through a regime of property, the decentralization of access to the means of production but on the different ways in which such an economy

---

*I return to this problem in greater detail in the next section.

can arrange the relations between private enterprise and governmental initiative.

There should be a heavy presumption against outlawing a practice on the ground that it represents a subsidy. Only when the government directly and immediately intervenes, and spends, in an effort to change the cost structure of exporting firms and to distort the commercial relations that would otherwise prevail, is there reason to prevent the intervention. Even then, the preferred remedy is not outright prohibition but the provision of a range of negotiated compensatory measures, all the way from trade favors accorded, in another department, to the foreign countries and businesses that may have been harmed to outright payment to the governments of such nations.

The reasons for the reversal of the presumption against subsidies that is favored by the emerging system of universal free trade are deep. They go to the root concerns motivating institutional minimalism about the organization of market economies.

For one thing, we have seen that what statically may appear to be the trumping of a market-based allocation by a government-commanded one may dynamically be something entirely different. It may represent an early move in the reorganization of the market in some sector. The market may need to be reorganized to be made more inclusive. Radical reform of the agricultural and credit markets in the nineteenth-century United States provides classic examples.

The problem presented by an attempt to distinguish the mere trumping of the present market allocation from the creation of another market, and therefore of another market allocation, is aggravated by a conundrum of prospective and retrospective insight. We may often be unable to tell beforehand which is which— market suppression or market reorganization: only success in reorganizing the market, especially to the end of making it more inclusive, will prove the point. However, failure will not suffice to justify us in casting the failed initiative as a mere subsidy; many failures may be needed to produce one success. The point, as Karl Popper said of mistakes in science, will be to make them as quickly as possible.

For another thing, the whole history of the economic rise of nations in the modern world is a history of the political construction of economic advantage, through everything from war to compensatory public investment. What the public investment compensates at the early stages of growth, in the economy as a whole or in one of its sectors, may be a localized market failure. It may also, and more commonly, be the inhibition to growth resulting from the relative scarcity of the resources, the facilities, the incitements, and the skills that would be more densely available in a more developed economy.

The apparent subsidy may be the *deus ex machina* that makes it possible to go from almost nothing to something. For richer countries to proscribe such compensatory investment as outlawed subsidies would indeed amount to kicking away the ladder on which they rose.

As with the first proposal—to put the reconciliation of alternative development trajectories within a progressively more open world economy in place of the maximization of free trade as the organizing principle of international commerce—so this second proposal will seem revolutionary or not, according to the assumptions with which one approaches it.

The implicit dominant view in most established economic thinking is that a market economy must have a foreordained institutional content if it is to do the work of efficient signaling and allocation that such thinking assigns to it. One part of this necessary institutional content will be a regime of private property and contractual freedom similar to the one that emerged in the course of modern European history. Another part is a wall separating the state from the individual or the firm, and governmental action or public policy from private enterprise.

It will be conceded, in this dominant view, that particular rules and arrangements may differ according to the prevailing legal tradition. It will also be admitted that room exists for a significant margin for variation, especially in the relative importance of the market and the state. When it regulates, redistributes, or even produces, government diminishes, according to this simple hydraulic conception, the power of the market to shape resource allocation according to its inner workings. However, such variations do nothing to change the fundamental institutional content of a market economy.

This view becomes explicit and is openly defended in only one of the major styles of economic thought: the one labeled in the earlier chapter on comparative advantage the strategy of pretension, with its aggressive advocacy of a particular institutional program as the intrinsic nature of the market economy and an indispensable backdrop to economic and political freedom. The same view, however, is left unchallenged by the other leading styles of economic thinking. The purists take refuge in their analytic agnosticism. The equivocators deploy what they refuse to defend, accepting, by default and without quarrel, the identification of the rational—the idea of the market—with the real—the narrow range of varieties of market economy that came to prevail in the course of modern Western history.

Any departure from the sole recognized type of market economy will fall under suspicion of representing a slide into *dirigisme,* into one or another way of meddling with the market and of trumping the allocation of resources at which the market would arrive were it able to operate perfectly. The case for regulation will seem to depend on the need to redress a "market failure," compensating for its consequences until its causes can be remedied. The idea that what is statically a subsidy—an allocation of resources overriding the actual or idealized market allocation—may dynamically amount to an early move in the reorganization of the market (to make the market, for example, more inclusive socially) will appear to be unintelligible or fallacious. Talk of alternative regimes of private and social property coexisting experimentally within the same economy will seem dangerous, if not futile. Such talk will be mistaken for an unacknowledged attack on the private law categories lying at the heart of the market economy.

Considered from the vantage point of this view, in any of its variations, an insistence that the rules of international trade not require adherence to any particular version of the market economy may seem to offer little benefit in return for real detriment. There seems to be little benefit because there is no prospect of worthwhile and fundamental reconstruction of the market economy. There appears to be real detriment because the attempt to act as if there were alternative market economies (as distinguished from limited "varieties of capitalism") will provide cover for distortions of trade as well as for restraints on the market. Toleration of subsidies may exemplify both these evils.

The significance of the minimalism about markets in this second proposal for the reformation of world trade changes entirely if we come to it armed with the belief that such alternatives are feasible and necessary. In this contrasting view, the established forms of the market economy prevent the anarchic experimentalism of the market from being radicalized. They keep the freedom to combine factors of production from turning into a more far-reaching power to recombine the components of the institutional setting of production and exchange. They frustrate the worldwide desire to achieve a form of economic growth that would be anchored in a great and irreversible expansion of economic opportunity. They make the goal of expanding access to the means of production hostage to the eternity and the absoluteness of the conventional property right. They represent a setting hostile to the propagation throughout the economy of the advanced practices of innovation-friendly cooperation beyond the boundaries of the advantaged and advanced sectors in which these practices are most likely to flourish. They are the beneficiaries of superstition working in the service of inhibition and injustice.

International trade should not be organized either to reinforce these established forms of the market economy or to impose any particular alternative to them. It should be organized to be as neutral as possible in the contest about them. It should avoid turning their adversaries into opponents of the shared effort to develop an open global economy.

Ideas and institutional innovations that would deepen democracy, democratize market economies, and enhance the educational and economic endowments of individuals lend greater interest and power to these proposals for the revision of the world economic order.* So, too, do ideas about alternative trajectories of national economic development. Both sets of ideas suggest how much we stand to gain by insisting that an open world economy be in fact open to the emergence of institutional and development alternatives as well as to the movement of goods and services.

It is nevertheless vital to the integrity and the authority of such proposals that the case for them not depend on commitment to any particular set of such alternatives. Instead of lending its force to the contested idea that the world does and should converge on a single version of the market economy, and indeed of democracy and liberty, the global trading regime should help let the future go free. It should remain as neutral as possible in the contest among alternative visions of the social future. In the same way and for the same reasons, it should struggle for impartiality in the contest between the view that the universal orthodoxy should be qualified by local heresies and the conviction that it can and should be resisted by a heresy that is as universalizing as the orthodoxy it opposes.

If there are no valuable alternatives, this liberating minimalism will help discredit them all the more quickly, preventing the ghostlike remnants of inherited ideological fantasy from distracting us from the only reliable path of advance. If there are valuable alternatives to be identified and developed, this worldwide experiment in the making of difference will not merely help reveal them; it will help make them.

Free Trade Reformed: Free Movements of Things and Money Chastened, Free Movement of People and Ideas Enhanced

The third plank in the platform of this program for the reform of the world trade regime is a radical change in the relations among

*I develop such ideas in two programmatic works, *Democracy Realized: The Progressive Alternative*, Verso, 1998, and *What Should the Left Propose?*, Verso, 2005.

free trade in goods and services, free flows of capital, and free movement of people. My earlier discussion anticipates the implications of this change as well as its justification.

The enhancement of opportunities for free flows of capital should be entirely disconnected from the development of free trade. When a country may have reason to restrict these flows as part of its effort to raise a shield over heresy is likely to be a matter of circumstance. The occasions to restrict the inward and outward movement of money may be far more common in the situations of relative advantage: those in which a country, within striking range of some of its major trading partners, finds itself engaged in the early stages of its effort to work out a rebellious and original strategy of national development. Thus, not by imposed rule but by a foreseeable concatenation of circumstance, a temporary retreat from free trade may coincide with an ephemeral restraint on the movement of money. In the long run, the cause of free flows of capital may be better served than harmed by a regime that avoids requiring those who would advance that cause to wear a straitjacket of conformity.

The place accorded in established dogma to sympathy for the movement of capital should be given instead to the movement of people. Such a bias should be built into the multilateral procedures, arrangements, and rules in which the emerging regime of world trade has its life. It should be a presumption, although one that can be rebutted.

The gradual strengthening of the right of labor to cross national frontiers is a direct inference from the ideas and assumptions justifying confidence in the market as a way of allocating and combining resources. It is also, by a long shot, the most effective contribution to the diminishment of inequality among nations.

If the enfranchisement of labor mobility were to be pursued too quickly or incautiously, its advantages would soon be overwhelmed by the vast disturbances and reactions it would trigger: the worsening of the position of relatively unskilled labor and of the rights of labor in general in the richer countries, the unbearable burden imposed on the already overburdened regimes of social security and entitlement in those same countries, the weakening of the almost tribal loyalties and identifications that, in many smaller and comparatively homogenous social democracies, have helped sustain support for the social-democratic settlement of the recent past, and the loss of scarce skilled talent by the countries of emigration.

Each of these real or potential problems, however, can yield to the cumulative effect of prudent dosage: for example, the sequencing of temporary work permits, partial social entitlements, and full social and political rights. Such a sequence would be accompanied by provisions to compensate the countries that lose skilled workers on whose education and training they have had to lavish resources they cannot easily replace. These precautionary and gradualist measures, when combined with the immense inertial forces of attachment and habit that dissuade all but the most restless from foreign adventures, should suffice to moderate the dangers of greater labor mobility while enabling the whole world to seize some of its benefits.

First among the formidable practical obstacles to the enhancement of labor's freedom to move are the threat to the position of labor and to the level of social entitlements in the receiving countries and the loss of educated talent in the sending countries. There are, however, solutions to these daunting problems. Immigrants can be admitted in slowly growing numbers. They can acquire social and political rights in successive tiers. Countries losing educated workers can be compensated for the investment in the skills of skilled labor by countries gaining them.

The remedies of gradualism and compensation in turn mitigate a more fundamental danger: that the increasing presence of the stranger, weakening the sense of cultural homogeneity and national cohesion, may erode the basis of whatever, by way of practical social solidarity, the existing social democracies have achieved. A considerable body of evidence supports the view that an active sense of responsibility for other people—and for other people's children—transcends only with difficulty the loyalties of the tribe.

It is true that European social democracy flourished during the twentieth century in a setting marked by national identification and ethnic unity. In that setting, it proved easier than it might otherwise have been to include "my fellow citizen" in the answer to the question, who is my brother? Yet even the most tribal of the European social democracies is not, and never was, a family writ large: in each instance, the sense of reciprocal attachment was forged on the basis of shared responsibility and common purpose. Democracy must multiply opportunities for such nation-creating experiences: the richer and the deeper these experiences become, the more capable they are of drawing in the stranger. To be able to bear more strangeness is an aspect of being more open to the new, and greater openness to the new is one of the most important attributes of the advance of a democratic society and of the culture that sustains it.

Thus, in reflecting on the difficulties that must be surmounted for labor to gain larger freedom of movement to cross national frontiers, it is not enough to deal with the threat such freedom poses to the workers of the North and to the societies of the South. It is necessary as well as to confront the challenge it presents to the established idea of nationality. The value of difference among nations in a world of democracies is to allow humanity to develop its powers by developing them in different directions: distinct forms of life, embodied in characteristic practices and institutions. Under democracy, prophecy must speak louder than memory. The distinction of nations becomes, in such a world, an inspiration to moral variety within humanity.

According to one of the fundamental and false premises of liberal political theory, a liberal democracy should distinguish between the impersonal right established in its institutions and its laws and the controversial views of the good that its individual citizens embrace. The truth, however, is that no such distinction can be sustained. It is a virtue of a democratic society to open itself to a broad range of human experience and possibility. Every institutional order, however, encourages some forms of experience and discourages others. The pursuit of a mirage of neutrality among different visions of the good—a tenet of classical liberal doctrine—gets in the way of the struggle to achieve the real goal of experimental openness to difference, contest, and novelty.

The encouragement of moral specialization within humanity, embodied in divergent sets of institutions, would undermine freedom and thus democracy itself, if it failed to ensure, as a counterpart or condition, the right of the individual to escape the society in which he happens to have been born and to join another. He must not be bound, by the accident of his birth, to a moral specialization with which he may lack sympathy. For this reason, the right to move is closely related to the value of the political partition of humanity.

These remarks suggest why the principle granting freedom to things (and to capital by analogy to things) but denying it to people should be replaced, and what should replace it. What should substitute for that invidious dogma is a predisposition progressively to expand the right of people to cross national frontiers. It is a predisposition that should remain subject to the prudential care to achieve even large advances in small steps. It should be qualified by the judgment of circumstance and opportunity.

Selective and temporary constraints on the movement of money may sometimes help a country take the initial steps in the execution of a rebellious strategy of national development. They may hasten rather than postpone the day when it can have a fully convertible currency. Because such restrictions on capital flows may form part of the initiatives composing the shield over heresy in development (as discussed earlier), they may help place a developing country in a position in which it no longer needed to pay for a convertible currency the price of renouncing any such resistance. A limited and superficial openness will not need to be achieved at the cost of a more general and fundamental freedom. Freedom of movement for money is an expedient, often useful and sometimes temporarily dangerous, its significance and effect fully shaped by the context in which it is deployed. By contrast, freedom of movement for people is a matter of principle, closely connected with the chief advantages of a market economy, subject to circumstantial constraint, and pregnant with immense practical consequence.

The movement gradually to establish a universal right of labor to cross national frontiers depends for its force and integrity on the continuance of a transformation already underway throughout much of the planet: the recasting of the differences among nations into a principle of moral differentiation rather than of quasi-biological succession. A world in which a devotion to the rights, the endowments, and the capabilities of the individual is combined with a vast expansion of the opportunity for difference and distinction in forms of collective life provides a much better background to the advancement of a reformed system of global free trade than one in which free trade depends on national conformity and institutional convergence. And a world in which every individual can, at the limit, escape his accidental birth in a social and cultural world he rejects, and make his sympathies triumph over his fate, will be more hospitable to the permanent creation of the new than one in which people are denied that freedom.

Free Trade Reformed: From Wage Slavery to Free Labor

The fourth principle on which a reformed system for universal free trade should rest is that its arrangements be designed to help free labor become free in fact. They should help diminish the extent to which free labor continues, because of economic duress, to resemble the slavery and the serfdom that it was meant to replace. At stake is the status of work and of workers under the world division of labor and the practical content of the legal status of free labor.

I have argued that of the three forms free labor can assume—wage labor, self-employment, and partnership—only the last two, or some combination of them, completes the break with slavery and realizes fully the idea of a market economy. Partnership enjoys an advantage over self-employment as a basis for cooperation capable of exploiting economies of scale. Wage labor, however, remains everywhere the dominant form of free labor. The question now before us is whether the development of an open world economy will be built on assumptions and arrangements that either limit or aggravate the features of wage labor that render it an incomplete and suspect realization of the ideal of free work.

It matters to every aspect of our experience and our future that free labor be really free. It matters to humanity's revelation to itself as context-transcending spirit. It matters not least to the character of the market economy. It is one thing for the contractual form of the relation between employers and employees to be real, and another thing for it be a feint. It matters to the likely forms of our future economic and social arrangements if labor in its present expressions is closer to slavery and serfdom or further away from them.

The most immediate means to the end of making free labor really free is the linkage of trade to labor standards. By the terms of this linkage, the global, regional, and bilateral arrangements establishing free trade are conditioned on an acceptance of standards ensuring that free wage work will become increasingly less like slavery and serfdom. By the terms of the basic deal that would enshrine this linkage, poorer, less productive countries would commit themselves to uphold ever more exacting labor standards in exchange for access to the markets of richer countries as well as for an overturning of barriers to the free flow of ideas throughout the world. Prominent among such barriers are those imposed by the present legal regime of intellectual property.

There are good reasons to establish in small, successive steps the free movement of people throughout the world. There are, however, no good reasons to limit, even temporarily, the free movement of ideas. The movement of things should be judged beneficial to humanity to the extent that it is based on arrangements inviting the movement of ideas and people. The movement of ideas and people overpowers in material and moral significance the movement of things; the single most important consideration in assessing the organization of the latter is its relation to the organization of the former.

A definition of the labor standards that would serve as the object of linkage should today include four elements and a horizon of development. This definition represents only a modest enhancement of ideas that have already begun to command authority throughout the world.

A first element in the applicable labor standards is the prohibition of all forms of slavery or forced labor, overt and covert, that deny the freedom of the worker to sell or to refuse to sell his labor. The same prohibition applies to all circumstances in which the factual presuppositions of individual self-determination are missing or gravely deficient and the physical or moral integrity of the individual is placed in jeopardy. Thus, child labor must be forbidden. So must circumstances of extreme danger or exertion unless the worker, fully informed of them and not driven to accept them by fear or necessity, chooses to face them in return for extraordinary compensation.

A second element is the outlawing of all forms of arbitrary discrimination in the allocation of employment and remuneration. Workers must not be placed and paid according to prejudices without reasonable relation to the value of the tasks they accomplish. The acceptance of arbitrary classifications among workers creates a situation antagonistic to recognition of the context-transcendent personality of the individual worker. It diminishes the distance of free labor from slavery or serfdom by treating individuals as destined to a type of work or compensation by virtue of membership in a social category from which they are powerless to escape regardless of the worth of what they can do or learn.

A third element is a living wage. The worker must receive a wage that enables him to sustain his own life and the lives of his dependents with the minimum degree of personal dignity that is recognized and required in the circumstances of his time, his community, and his society. Suppose, exceptionally, that his country is too poor and unproductive to assure him of such a wage. Suppose that it cannot do so even when its adherence to labor standards is rewarded by greater access to the markets of rich countries as well as to their ideas, practices, and inventions. In such a circumstance, the supplementary remuneration of the worker or the enhancement of the productivity of his labor becomes the responsibility of the entire world. Failure to obtain a living wage amounts once again to a shortening of the distance between free labor and slavery: extreme economic necessity threatens to make a travesty of the contractual form of the employment relation and to rob the worker of the practical requirements of independent economic and moral agency.

The fourth element is a way of organizing the relations between capital and labor and, more broadly, the political life of the people that allows there to be a peaceful contest over the terms on which labor will be sold. The premise of such arrangements is that dependent wage labor is itself a defective form of free labor and one that represents an unfinished break from slavery. The right of association—the right to organize and to strike—is the most immediate and familiar expression of this requirement.

Just as there should be experimentation with the forms of the market economy, so too there should be experimentation with the forms of association. The most effective type of union organization may, for example, be one combining the corporatist principle of automatic unionization of all workers in an economy with the contractualist principle of complete freedom to stake out different positions within the union structure that is established. Rival labor movements, connected or not with political parties, would compete for position in this structure just as political parties compete for a place in the structure of government. Automatic unionization would shift the focus of energy away from whether to associate and toward how to use the power resulting from association, to the benefit of the economically weakest segments of a national labor force. It would give a solidaristic and inclusive tilt to negotiation between employers and employees, inhibiting the entrenchment of stark divisions between privileged insiders, holding well-paid jobs in the more capital-intensive, productive sectors of the economy, and disenfranchised outsiders, with unstable and poorly paid jobs in the capital-starved sectors of the economy. And, by its inclusiveness of membership and robustness, it would make it more likely for the concerns of the membership to go beyond economic claims and to focus on rights and institutions.

The advantages of association can be realized most completely only in the context of democracy, and indeed of an effort to combine traits of representative and direct democracy. The more organized and participatory a society, the greater is its power to envisage alternative futures and to work them out, and the greater the likelihood that the effort to make free labor really free will come to the center of social concern.

What the enfranchisement of labor cannot have as a measure of its sufficiency is success in obtaining any particular share in national income. There is no such algorithm. The dogma that the advance of the real wage must be tied to increases in the productivity of labor is, I have claimed, false, despite its widespread acceptance. The course of politics and the institutions of the economy and the polity will powerfully influence the part of national income accruing to labor. However, a persistent lag of the real wage behind productivity gains establishes a presumption of danger as well as of unfairness. Absence or weakness of an upward tilt to the wage means diminished pressure, in a sector of the economy or in an economy as whole, to climb the ladder of forms of economic life that are increasingly productive because they use repetitious machines to help people spend more time doing what they do not yet know how to repeat.

These four components of the labor standards that should be incorporated into the conditions of trade among nations are unified by the horizon toward which they advance. This horizon is the alleviation of the economic duress weighing on wage labor and the gradual replacement of wage labor, as the standard status of work, by self-employment or partnership. The substitution of self-employment and partnership for wage labor can be reconciled with imperatives of scale and discretion in production only through a vast enlargement of the range of forms of private and social property.

The immediate occasion for this linkage of trade to labor standards is the need to address two major problems in the contemporary world. The first problem is the threat to the situation of workers in the rich countries represented by the formation of a universal labor pool, most especially by the arrival of vast masses of poor but increasingly skilled workers in China and India. The second problem is the constraint on which labor is placed in the developing countries to compensate for low total factor productivity by continuing repression of the wage take from national income. This repression passes, at the limit, into forms of oppression and subjugation that diminish the difference between wage labor and slavery.

A partial response to these two problems at once is to incorporate into the legal conditions of free trade the labor standards I have described, with their ultimate movement away from wage labor to self-employment and partnership. The poorer countries would agree to such standards, according to this response, in return for greater access to the markets of the rich countries and to the ideas and inventions that emanate from them. (I later consider what this greater access to ideas and inventions requires.) The case for the incorporation, however, transcends its immediate justifications: the interest and the ideal on which it rests is the building of an open world economy on the basis of free labor and the completion of the struggle to expunge from free work the remnants of slavery that continue to taint it.

Past experience suggests that the deal of labor standards for market access and for accessibility to ideas and inventions may have two opposite sets of practical effects.

On the one hand, it may impose an upward pressure on the returns to labor, providing an incitement to climb more quickly in the scale of the dialectic between our repetitious and our not yet repeatable activities. It would then be as if the whole of humanity had been lifted into a higher key of productivity and ambition.

On the other hand, however, it may also help throw some economies into a trap of high unit-labor costs. The effective cost of labor may increase while productivity fails to rise accordingly. The Mexican situation, cited earlier, exemplifies such an outcome: labor costs that can never be as low as those of the major economies in which work is cheapest but without the productivity gains that even some of those cheap-labor countries (China, India) have achieved—gains in total factor productivity as well as in labor productivity. This productivity trap has been set without any linkage of labor standards to trade having been established. The increase of wage costs resulting from the linkage might, however, worsen it; the enhancement of the status of labor may fail to result in an enhancement of either labor or total factor productivity.

Two sets of influences, one distinguishing paths of national development, the other characterizing the arrangements of the world economic order, make it more likely for the benign outcome to prevail—the ascent rather than the trap. These internal and external influences may help perpetuate a permanent revolution in productivity.

The internal influences can in turn be divided into three categories of initiatives. Each of them has been explored in earlier parts of this book.

One set of influences has to do with the shield raised over heresy in the choice of strategies of national development. A government must reject the latter-day functional equivalent to the late nineteenth-century gold standard: the syndrome of low domestic saving; heavy dependence on foreign capital; unconditional freedom for capital to come and go; weak links between saving and production; management of the public debt in the interest of rentiers to the detriment of the interests of workers and entrepreneurs; fiscal discipline achieved by cuts in public spending and investment rather than by sustained increases in the tax take; and, in general, abdication of any national strategy. These ideas and arrangements have the effect of tying the hands of the government and subjecting it to the whims and vetoes of the domestic and global capital markets. They amount to a self-inflicted emasculation. Instead, the government should mobilize the natural, financial, and human resources of the nation, reversing each of the elements of this syndrome of surrender. At the limit, it should organize a war economy without a war.

A second series of attributes of the national direction that can increase the likelihood of the benign result is that it be marked by a commitment to make the market economy more inclusive by reorganizing it. The commanding goal must be the expansion of economic and educational opportunity. The broadening of economic opportunity will repeatedly require innovations in the terms by which people acquire claims to productive resources, and thus ultimately in the regimes of contract and property.

Such innovations will include changes in the ways in which private enterprise can coexist with governmental policy. They cannot rest content with the choice presented by the American model of arm's length regulation of business by government and the imposition of unified industrial policy by a central bureaucracy. The innovations should also make it easier for private producers to pool resources at the same time that they compete, developing networks of cooperative competition.

Public initiative should be used to counteract the inhibitions of relative backwardness and to make up for the difficulty in that circumstance of using one line of production to open up another. However, this help, intended to arouse a fever of entrepreneurial activity, should be accompanied by the selective mechanisms of competition, winnowing out its better and worse results. If foreign competition is limited by the qualifications that apply to the introduction of free trade, domestic competition should be made all the more vigorous.

The widening of educational opportunity requires a school that rescues the child from the family as well as from the state and that assures him mastery of a core of generic practical and conceptual capabilities. It calls for an education faithful to the experimentalist ideal in its focus on problem solving and analysis rather than information, its cooperative rather than authoritarian and individualistic setting, its preference for selective deepening over encyclopedic scope, and its devotion to dialectic over all dogma.

A third group of incitements to a continued rise in total factor productivity is the opening of the gateways of access to the advanced sectors of production: those that are characterized less by the accumulation of capital and technology than by the propagation of the practices of innovation-friendly cooperation. The turning of production into permanent innovation, the mixture of cooperation and competition and the attenuation of rigid divisions between conception and implementation, as well as among implementing roles, must not be allowed to flourish solely in the favored conditions of advanced sectors only weakly linked to the rest of the economy. These practices must be spread beyond their expected place—the vanguards of production. They must be introduced before their expected time—the achievement of developed country status. They must advance and spread without a blueprint—by the organized contagion of decentralized inspiration rather than the contrived scheming of an all-knowing power. None of this can occur except by making it happen, through forms of governmental initiative and social action. Such initiatives make up for the absence, in many relatively more backward countries or in the more backward sectors of the most advanced economies, of the conditions favoring this productive vanguardism: exacting education and high trust.

The chief international condition that would help turn the elevation of labor standards into an incitement to a continuing rise in total factor productivity rather than a productivity trap is the free flow of ideas and inventions throughout the world. (Mechanical inventions are no more than ideas embodied in things, the rule-like formulas in which we can express repetitious labor and the physical contraptions in which we can embody such formulas.) The result of this freedom would be to diminish the reality of one of the assumptions on which Ricardo based the doctrine of comparative advantage: the distinction among the technologies of production available to different countries.

What was said of the scientific ambitions of the members of the Royal Society in seventeenth-century England should be repeated of every member of the world trading system: "[they] ought to have their eyes in all parts, and to receive information from every quarter of the earth, they ought to have a constant universal intelligence; all discoveries should be brought to them. . ."*

The effective availability of the ideas and inventions of the whole world in every part of the world would not automatically cause a worldwide revolution in productivity; there are many steps between even an idea that has already been housed in a machine and its effective use of that mechanical invention. Nevertheless, it would vastly increase the prospect for such a revolution and for its efficacy as a continuing force rather than as a one-time event.

The most burdensome obstacle to this outcome is the established legal regime of intellectual property. Today the richest countries seek to extend and to enforce this regime throughout the planet as a condition of world free trade and an inherent feature of the type of market economy they seek to make universal.

---

*Thomas Sprat, *The History of the Royal Society*, edited by Jackson I. Cope and Harold Whitmore Jones, London: Routledge & Kegan Paul, 1959, p. 20.

They insist on seeing this regime incorporated into all multilateral, regional, and bilateral arrangements. The development of an open world economy should instead be accompanied by radical revision of this regime.

The structure of the argument for the established way of protecting intellectual property parallels the structure of the defense of the hereditary transmission of property. The difference lies only in the outcome: in one instance, a loss to equality of opportunity; in the other, a harm to the common interest of mankind in rendering work throughout the world less repetitious and more productive.

In both controversies, two distinct arguments are deployed and combined: one from natural right, the other from indispensable incentives. The first argument is from prepolitical or natural right: the legitimacy of the right, whether to inherit or to charge a rent for the use of an invention, would result from an unbroken succession of entitlements. Nothing but the legitimate origin of the right and the legitimate chain of transactions marking its life could, in this view, ground the entitlement of the present rightholder.

All such argument from natural right shares in the character of an enslaving superstition: it naturalizes the arrangements of society by denying or radically underestimating the contingent and constructed character of the property right and the variety of ways, each of them with very different consequences for society, in which effort can be rewarded. It also misplaces the source of concern for the empowerment of the individual and for his protection against all forms of governmental and private oppression in privileges that become themselves devices of exclusion and subjugation. What is crucial is that the individual be secure in a haven of vital safeguards and economic and educational endowments not dependent on holding any particular job or place in society. Such safeguards and endowments are the sole reliable basis for his ability to resist, change, and transcend the settings within which he acts.

If the argument from natural right is fallacious, the argument from incentives is incomplete and inconclusive. The right of inheritance would be necessary as an incentive to energy and effort.

The exclusionary protection of intellectual property through the patent system, with its establishment of a legal monopoly, would be required to remunerate the large risks and investments, of money and time, needed to finance invention in the long process from speculative conjecture to practical realization.

It is a real, not a sham, argument. However, its weight depends on the nature of the accessible alternative ways to achieve the same incentive with less collateral harm. Can the allowance of only modest family inheritance preserve the major part of the incentive effects of the hereditary transmission of property, given that the accumulation of wealth is attended by a host of advantages, of power and preeminence, that do not depend for their force on a right to enrich one's heirs? Can a system of public rewards and subsidies—like the ones tried out and suppressed in the nineteenth century—provide much of what is needed by means of encouragement to invention? Or can nonexclusive and limited claims to the returns, such as a venture capitalist might enjoy in enterprises he helps finance, ensure the desired effect when rewards and subsidies prove insufficient?

The bad argument from natural right and the inconclusive argument from incentives are not turned into a good and conclusive argument by being, as they in practice are, indistinctly combined, the weakness of each one disguised by the appeal to the other.

We have a large stake in finding practical alternatives to a legal regime that inhibits people around the world from sharing more fully in the products of human ingenuity and that threatens to diminish the value of free labor as an incitement to permanent revolution in both total factor and labor productivity.

Consider now, in the light of the previous three counterprinciples, this fourth counterprinciple to the principles governing the regime of world trade. The overt subject of this book has been the movement of things across national boundaries. One of its covert subjects has been the movement of people and ideas across those same frontiers. The most that we can hope of the movement of things is that it be sometimes useful, although we must recognize that it is sometimes harmful.

The movement of people and ideas is vastly more useful than the movement of things as a source of greater equality, as well as of greater wealth and power, for all mankind. Both the movement of people and the movement of ideas have the potential to make a contribution to economic growth as well as to economic or technological innovation, that overpowers any contribution we have received, or can ever expect, from the worldwide movement of things. Both the movement of people and the movement of ideas have built into them an irresistible equalizing force: through the workings of each of them, economic growth and social equality can be allied rather than opposed.

The movement of people and ideas is, however, more than useful; it is sacrosanct. It forms part of the process by which the whole human race becomes both one and diverse, and makes itself more godlike, by affirming in the individual as well as in the species, its preeminence over the particular social and cultural worlds that it builds and inhabits. Both the movement of people and the movement of ideas can unsettle and frighten us, driving us back into ourselves. They can also inspire us to reimagine and to remake our interests, our ideals, and even our identities by beginning to detach them from the settings with which we habitually associate them. Each of them is therefore an invitation to open ourselves to the new, in a world in which every man and woman has a better chance to become the original that he imagines himself to be.

It follows from this line of reasoning that one of the most important standards by which to judge when the movement of things is either useful or harmful is to determine when it either advances the movement of people and ideas or sets it back. To attribute to the movement of things the sanctity that properly belongs to the movement of people and ideas is more than an economic and political mistake; it is a spiritual perversion, tainted by idolatry, the confusion of living, transcendent, and embodied spirit with lifeless objects.

The same way of thinking exemplified by this linkage between trade and labor standards should be extended by analogy to the connection between trade and standards for the protection of nature. The distinctive character of the problem, however, requires that the linkage have features that are absent from the linkage to labor standards.

Some of the reasons to incorporate environmental standards into trade agreements are familiar. They work to prevent the spread of unsustainable forms of economic growth. They have the potential to unite humanity in the defense of a universal interest, including the avoidance of destructive climate change. They are a requirement of justice among generations, preventing the enrichment of the living from being achieved at the cost of depriving the unborn of the spiritual as well as the material advantages of nature less spoiled. There are, however, further reasons to link trade to environmental standards.

One such reason is that the pressure to produce and to grow under the restraint of protection of nature may also encourage technological and organizational innovation and contribute to a permanent revolution in productivity. The depredation of nature is not only a wrong that we do to ourselves and to our descendants; it is also an easy escape from the pressure to do more with less, as if we were to pillage nature to avoid taxing our own ingenuity.

Once again, however, the increased pressure may have two opposite outcomes: a strengthened impulse toward a sustained rise in total factor as well as labor productivity or a further descent into a low-productivity trap. The burden and the danger are likely to fall most heavily on the developing countries, which are least able to bear them. Once again, this likelihood requires that these countries be compensated for their adherence to environmental standards by enhanced access to the markets of the rich economies as well as to the ideas and inventions of the whole world. Such compensations, however, may well prove inadequate. They need to be supplemented in two ways.

A first supplement is the use of an increasing scale. The standards should be related to gross categories of development and productivity, beginning low and becoming more demanding as the country rises in this ranking. If the world, especially the rich world, wants a faster schedule, it should pay to obtain it, with outright cash transfers as well as with enhanced market access. Moreover, it will have no basis on which to propose a sliding scale of environmental standards to the developing countries if, within itself, it contains powers that resist the application of such a sliding scale to themselves (the case of the United States today).

A second supplement addresses the issue presented when there is interest in restricting, for the benefit of humanity, the form of development of an entire region located within an individual country. It is the extreme form of a pervasive problem; an unequal sacrifice to secure a universal benefit. A similar difficulty may arise more obliquely when the environmental restraints fall on a range of technologies or businesses for which a particular country may be especially well suited by established comparative advantage. In all such instances, the same generic solution may be appropriate: the world should pay with increased market access or straightforward cash transfers.

The usefulness of such a solution lies in its promise of extending the opportunity to safeguard common interests of the partners in a global trading system while minimizing the restraints on experimental diversity among the partners. Both the aim and the method can apply to matters far beyond the scope of environmental concerns.

A final justification of the linkage between trade and environmental standards remains. It goes to the heart of the view of humanity animating the argument of this book. The central idea in this view is that we are greater, individually as well as collectively, than the social and cultural worlds we build and inhabit. For us, there can be no final frame of reference, an institutional or conceptual context that could serve as our definitive home and accommodate the varieties of experience that we have power to create and reason to value. The impossibility of such a definitive frame of reference has two large implications.

The first implication is that we have an interest in creating institutional and conceptual structures that, by facilitating their own revision, enable us to split the difference between being inside them and being outside them. This change in the relation of structural restraint to structure-defying freedom is the next best thing to the all-inclusive and insuperable frame of reference for which we cannot and should not hope.

The second implication is that we must make ourselves different from one another, both as collectivities and as individuals, if we are to make ourselves greater. Humanity can develop its powers only by developing them in different directions and by housing contrasting forms of life in distinct institutional orders.

To complicate our relation to nature is to find yet another encouragement to this indispensable and transformative diversification. If our relation to nature is restricted to a choice between depredation and delight, between nature as fuel, to be pillaged and used, and nature as garden, to succor and distract, our dealings with the natural setting of our lives in society will provide little occasion to reinvent ourselves.

Suppose, however, that we arrange our economic life, in the separate states in which humanity remains divided and in the world as a whole, to favor a multiplication of ways of dealing with nature that escape the contrast between instrumental use and noninstrumental engagement. These mixed forms will inspire, indeed they will demand, new forms of social and economic organization. The protection of nature will then have supported diversity as well as efficiency; it will have helped inspire the reinvention of society.

The Troubles of Free Trade and
the Possibilities of Economics

● ○ ●

This book may be misread as a polemic against free trade. It is not. Its immediate concern is to propose a change in how we understand the benefits and dangers of trade among countries. The understanding I put forward results in a view of how to build an open world economy without harming some of our most important material and moral interests. If my proximate goal here is to reimagine free trade, my ulterior motive is to argue for a change in the way we think about markets, the division of labor, and the relation of production and exchange to the rest of our social experience.

It is impossible to develop and to state this view of international commerce without expanding—even radically—the scope of the traditional analysis, not just of trade but of economic life in general, and casting off some of the assumptions on which this analysis has rested.

One of these assumptions has to do with insight into the relation between the abstract idea of a market, whether domestic or global, and the detailed legal and institutional arrangements through which this idea must be realized. There is simply no straightforward passage from one to the other. A national market economy may be organized in an open-ended number of very different ways, with very different consequences for the economic as well as the noneconomic aspects of social life. The same consideration applies as well to the conception of an open world economy. So long as we fail to take this truth to heart, or pretend to accept it in principle while disregarding it in our analytic and argumentative practice, our explanatory and programmatic ideas about free trade will remain in the shadow of unacknowledged and unwarranted preconceptions.

A second assumption deals with the political setting of economic decisions. No premise of the conventional way of thinking is more fateful for our approach to the identification of economic alternatives and therefore to the understanding of economic realities than a lack of imagination about the consequences of political institutions for economic alternatives. Because there is no single, natural form of a market economy and because no market economy can define its own institutional and ideological presuppositions, there can be no escape from political choice, not even in the organization and correction of the market, whether in a particular country or in the whole world.

But who is to be the agent capable of formulating a collective interest that transcends the self-interest of particular factions and classes in society? Who can choose the presuppositions without serving as the instrument for the specious and predatory imposition of factional and class interest on the whole of society through the power of the state? To say that this question has no answer is to abdicate the future of society not to the forces of the market— a phantasm of our superstitions—but rather to the interests predominant in the particular type of market order that happens to be established. To say that the answer to this question lies in the appeal to an enlightened despotism or despotic bureaucracy capable of lifting itself above the particular interests in contest is to make the future of society hostage to the ambitions and the prejudices of the would-be savior. It is to sacrifice collective discovery to dogma armed with power. To look for the answer to this question in a preestablished formula of democratic politics, such as the varieties of representative democracy now established in the rich North Atlantic countries, is to make about democracy the same mistake that the conventional thinking makes about markets, identifying the incomplete political ideal with its contingent and flawed institutional forms. Because these forms continue to inhibit the transformation of society through politics and to make change await crisis, they also allow some interests to continue ruling over others in the society and the economy.

There is only one acceptable answer to the question of who is to speak in economic policy and elsewhere for the public interest. It is to deepen democracy through institutions that raise the level of organized popular participation in politics, combining features of representative and direct democracy; favor the rapid resolution of impasse in government and policy; create procedures for disrupting and reorganizing the particular practices and organizations that give rise to entrenched social exclusion or disadvantage; enhance the capability-sustaining educational and economic endowments of individuals without making access to such endowments depend on holding any particular job; enable a society to hedge its bets by trying out, in particular sectors or localities, countermodels to its main line of evolution; and, in all these ways, diminish the dependence of change on calamity and weaken the power of the past over the future.

Such a radicalization of the principle of democratic experimentalism can be achieved only through renovation of the narrow repertory of institutional arrangements to which contemporary societies remain bound. One of its many benefits is to save us from having to deny ourselves recourse to policies requiring unequal treatment of different economic activities. It gives us practical means with which to answer the complaint that although such policies may be justified in theory, they will always be corrupt in practice. They will allow the powers of government to be usurped by self-serving interests.

The alternative to the fake perpetual-motion machine of a market order that never needs to be reimagined and remade, but only to benefit from localized corrections and compensations, is democracy, reimagined and remade. In this sense, some of the theoretical conundra of economics have only practical solutions. Such solutions, however, are not economic; they are political.

A third assumption concerns the character and virtues of the division of labor. International free trade, on the basis of established or constructed comparative advantage, is nothing but a special case of the division of labor. The images of Adam Smith's pin factory, with its regimen of hierarchical specialization, and of Karl Marx's reign of scarcity, in which the coercive extraction of the surplus remains the indispensable condition of practical progress, continue to shape our economic ideas. They penetrate, in countless unsuspected ways, the ideas of free traders and protectionists alike.

However, they have become ever less useful guides to understanding our situation. Not the pin factory, but the treadmill of perpetual innovation; not the coercive extraction of a surplus, but success in diffusing throughout social and economic life a revolutionary set of innovation-friendly practices of cooperation, have become the gateways to wealth. The future lies in using repeatable labor, expressed in formulas that are in turn embodied in machines, to save more of our most important resource, time, for the activities we have not yet learned to repeat. What seemed to be the main road in the history of specialization in production, exemplified by Smith's pin factory, has turned out to be only an early byway. Our view of the international division of labor must necessarily reflect our insight into the division of labor in general.

A fourth assumption has to do with the relation between the efficient allocation of resources at a static moment in time, on the basis of arrangements for the organization of the market and of the division of labor that we can take for granted, and the ability to continue experimenting with new institutions and practices as well as with new ways to do things within the current practices and institutions. The familiar contrast of static and dynamic efficiencies fails to do justice to the scope and depth of the problem. The point is to escape being arrested within approaches to the organization of both the market economy and the division of labor that limit, unnecessarily and unjustifiably, what Karl Marx called the development of the productive forces of society. The goal is to avoid surrendering to the necessitarian assumptions that tainted Marx's own theory of the relation between productive forces and economic institutions, with its conception of a foreordained sequence of modes of production, each of them an indivisible institutional system and all of them in sequence driven forward by inexorable laws of transformation. The aim is to develop the power to innovate in the forms of the market economy and of the division of labor themselves, without requiring crisis and calamity as conditions of change.

Our ideas about every national or worldwide regime for market-based exchange must always operate at two levels. At one level—the one at which economic analysis has traditionally worked—we consider only the freedom to trade goods and services and to combine, in their production, people, ideas, and things. At another level—the one at which a less superstitious way of thinking must learn to move—we look to the freedom to revise, piece by piece and step by step, the framework of institutional arrangements and assumptions within which we trade and combine. Our reasoning at the first level should be informed by our thinking at the second.

A set of arrangements, for a country or for the whole world, that seems fully to enact an ideal of free exchange, when viewed only at the first level, may appear intolerably and unnecessarily wanting when reconsidered at the second level. That is what happens with the plan now underway to establish a selective, invidious, and antiexperimentalist version of free trade as the capstone of a world economy. It is also what happens with the forms of the market economy that are now established in the most successful economies of the world and that are identified by all but the purest—and the emptiest—forms of economic analysis as the indispensable institutional instruments of efficient resource allocation. Pushed to the hilt, an insistence on thinking simultaneously at both these levels has the potential to revolutionize our attitudes to the established organization of market economies and to the present course of globalization.

It would be paradoxical and self-defeating for faith in a world market, developed under the banner of free trade, to result in a dogmatic constraint on our powers of decentralized and divergent experimentation. It is not good enough to experiment in production; we need to experiment as well with the forms of experimentation, globally as well as locally. Otherwise we betray the practical reasons that lead us to prefer economic decentralization to economic centralism in the first place.

A fifth assumption goes to the relation between efficiency and diversity. The dominant tradition of economic thought focuses on mechanisms for selecting the most efficient solutions to the problems of production and exchange. It takes for granted the diversification of the material—all the way from different goods and services to different technologies, practices, arrangements, and ideas—to which these selective mechanisms of efficiency apply. The inherited institutional framework of the market, occasionally adjusted, is treated as sufficient to ensure the requisite wealth of experiments in economic life.

We cannot, however, take the creation of diversity for granted. It is at least half of the work of economic progress. It is a task, not a given. In economic development it is necessary to arouse a fever of constructive entrepreneurial activity and to counteract the inhibitions and deficiencies of relative backwardness, and then to subject the results of this feverish activity to remorseless competitive selection. So, more generally, in the workings of an economy it is vital to ask at every turn both what will select and what will diversify: the imperatives efficiency and diversity have to be met, each in relation to the other.

This seemingly innocuous proposition requires us to reconsider many of our most cherished economic assumptions, including our assumptions about the benefits and dangers of international trade and the desirable route to the construction of an open world economy. It underlines the reasons for wanting alternative regimes of property and contract, and varied relations between government and private enterprise, to coexist experimentally within the same market economy. It also reveals the distinctly economic value of the political partition of mankind, the very premise of international trade and, at the same time, a subject about which trade theory, and economics as a whole, have strangely had little or nothing to say.

These considerations may seem unobjectionable when stated as abstractions. We cannot, however, take them seriously without changing both the way we think about world trade and the way we organize it.

In reimagining free trade, revision of the assumptions of our ideas about trade must be accompanied by expansion of the scope of these ideas. The value of institutional difference, the requirements of institutional innovation, the nature of the way in which we can renovate and enlarge the restricted repertory of institutional arrangements by which contemporary societies remain gripped, now that the calamitous ideological adventures of the twentieth century are spent—all these topics turn out to be vital to any effort to rise above the traditional terms of debate between free traders and protectionists.

Here we touch on the nature, the limits, and the agenda of economic theory as well as of the related social sciences. Ever since the rise of marginalism in the late nineteenth century, the preponderant orientation of economics has been to seek immunity from causal and normative controversy. Causal claims and normative assumptions alike must, on this formal, austere model of thought, be imported from outside the analytic apparatus. They form part of the boundary conditions or of the stipulations with which economic analysis must work.

The result is a method of thought that achieves explanatory and argumentative power only with the help of ideas that it is itself powerless to generate or to justify. It must borrow these ideas, as the conventional doctrine of free trade borrowed ideas about the division of labor that have turned out to be false. Its immunity is bought at the risk of vacuity. It will not even enjoy the power of pure mathematics—of Kant's synthetic a priori—to establish relations that are at once formal and surprising. Denied the capacity to understand the actual by understanding what, under the pressure of different initiatives and circumstances, the actual might become, such a practice of economic analysis will forever remain the somber discipline of constraints and trade-offs.

The intellectual alternative is not to dissolve rigorous analysis into an unbounded exploration of the subject matter of all the other social sciences. It is to return to the path that economics abandoned when it embraced the strategy of immunizing itself from controversial causal and prescriptive claims: to rediscover and redirect the road that it had traveled in the period from Smith to Marx. In that earlier way of thinking, economics had offered and justified a complex of causal ideas and social ideals. It had struggled to relate the production of things, the structures of society, and the powers of the mind.

We can no longer work on the premises of those premarginalist economists. Their thought suffered from an early form of the superstitions that continue to threaten ours: a radical understatement of the plurality of alternative institutional trajectories that the development of our productive powers can follow, an exaggeration, inimical to experimentalism as well as to democracy, of the need for hierarchy and specialization, a willingness to give the last word to history rather than to keep it for ourselves. Nevertheless, the effort to work in a vein less inclusive and ambitious than theirs has brought us to a dead end.

Our solution cannot resemble theirs in content. It should nevertheless resemble theirs in at least one trait of spirit. It should reject the strategy of immunization from causal and normative controversy and yet resist the danger of dissolution in the specificities of social science as well as in the generalities of political argument. It should seek to develop explanatory claims and prescriptive ideas relating different forms of production and exchange to different ways of organizing those who exchange and produce. It should connect the transformation of nature with the transformation of society, the making of things with the reorganization of people. It should represent the actual under the aegis of the possible, given that, in social study as in natural science, to understand a phenomenon or a state of affairs is to grasp what it can become under varying interventions or conditions of pressure.

The possible that matters is not the rationalistic idea of a closed horizon of possible worlds—possible forms of the market economy or of production and exchange under scarcity or of specialization and trade among trading partners. The possible that counts is the pragmatic conception of the adjacent possible: the next steps that we can take, the *there* that we can get to from *here*.

These remarks about method may seem too abstract to be useful, but the ideas of this book offer an applied example of what they mean.

Free trade—how to think about it and what to do about it—is far from being the largest problem now facing mankind. No contemporary issue, however, more strikingly combines theoretical interest with practical urgency. As fact, free trade gives voice to the two impulses that exercise the widest influence in the world today: the turn to markets and the advance of globalization. As doctrine, it supports the belief that we should rejoice in the workings of these twin impulses as well as resign ourselves to their triumph.

The established practice of international trade gives us cause to rebel until we reshape both market economies and globalization, not to reject the ideas of free exchange and of free labor but to radicalize them as bases for an open world economy. A changed theory of international trade gives us reason to reimagine until we see with new eyes the relation between constraint and possibility in the national and the world economies, and recover as transformative opportunity what we had mistaken for unyielding fate. We will not shackle humanity to free trade.

Name Index

● ○ ●

Subject Index

● ○ ●